CSF

Body c

Body and Soul

A Spirituality of Imaginative Creativity

FINTAN CREAVEN, SJ

First published in Great Britain in 2003 by
Society for Promoting Christian Knowledge
Holy Trinity Church
Marylebone Road
London NW1 4DU

The author and the publisher acknowledge with thanks permission to
reproduce the following extracts from:

'Snake' by D. H. Lawrence in *The Faber Book of Modern Verse*, ed. Michael
Roberts, Faber and Faber, 1965. Reproduced by permission of Pollinger Ltd
and the Estate of Frieda Lawrence Ravagli.
'Finn's Poem on Mayday' by Mary Low in *Celtic Christianity and Nature*,
Edinburgh University Press, 1996.
Blathmac's poem taken from *A World Made Whole* by Esther de Waal.
Copyright ©. Used by permission of Zondervan.

Every effort has been made to trace and acknowledge copyright
holders of material reproduced in this book. The publisher
apologizes for any omissions that may remain and, if notified, will
ensure that full acknowledgements are made in a subsequent edition.

Unless otherwise stated, Scripture quotations are adapted from
The Jerusalem Bible, published and copyright © 1966, 1967 and 1968
by Darton, Longman & Todd Ltd and Doubleday, a division of
Random House, Inc. and used by permission.
Scripture quotations from the New English Bible © Oxford University Press
and Cambridge University Press, 1961, 1970.

British Library Cataloguing-in-Publication Data
A catalogue record for this book is available from the British Library

ISBN 0–281–05524–6

1 3 5 7 9 10 8 6 4 2

Typeset by Pioneer Associates, Perthshire
Printed in Great Britain by
Bookmarque Ltd, Croydon, Surrey

Contents

Foreword

In recent decades New Age spirituality has been enjoying worldwide popularity. Without any apparent centralized organization, it appeals to people across nations and cultures. In many large bookshops there is now a large section called Spirituality, most of it New Age, occupying the ground floor, while Religion is relegated to a much smaller section upstairs. Mention of New Age causes shudders in some Christian circles, where it is often considered to be a reversion to paganism.

Why is New Age so popular? In spite of some of its zanier manifestations, New Age is in search of a spirituality which engages not spirit only, but body, mind and spirit, an emphasis which has been neglected in mainstream Christianity in recent centuries, leaving us with a split spirituality. We show great reverence for God in our places and style of worship, in our credal statements and church discipline, but we also take remarkable care not to let God interfere in our ordinary everyday affairs. This split affects every aspect of our lives: it causes a split within ourselves between our reason and emotion; it brings about a splintering in the Christian body, dividing us from one another, and from people of different faiths and of no faith; it divides us from the earth, source of all life. We are so divided that to preserve their national interests, the wealthy countries of the world have stores of nuclear weaponry, more than enough to destroy all life on earth. We exploit the world's resources at a rate which, if it continues, will ensure such pollution of the atmosphere and depletion of resources that our planet will no longer be able to sustain human life. While we know about these dangers, know that the greed of developed nations causes starvation in poor countries, our knowledge is so separated from our emotions that we fail to take effective action.

In *Body and Soul*, Fintan Creaven, a Celt and Jesuit, explores this split with his insights into the nature of Celtic spirituality, a spirituality of body, mind and spirit, at home with God who is at home on earth. Fintan's writing breathes and communicates the Celtic spirit of delight in creation, God's cloak, which we are continuously touching in our earthly life. He ends each chapter with a very Celtic touch, a poetic summary.

He also shows how these essential elements of Celtic spirituality also characterize Ignatius Loyola's *Spiritual Exercises*, written in the sixteenth century, a striking similarity which I have never seen in print before.

The Celtic nature of the *Spiritual Exercises* is not immediately obvious. One cannot imagine the single-minded Ignatius scribbling in the margin of his *Spiritual Exercises* manuscript, 'Pleasant is the glittering of the sun today upon these margins, because it flickers so,' as one Celtic scribe wrote in the margin of an important document he was copying. *Body and Soul* brings out the close affinity between the two spiritualities. The way in which we perceive the world determines our way of being in it, how we relate to ourselves, to one another, to all creation. Celtic and Ignatian spirituality offer the new way of seeing all reality as God's gift. Both spiritualities delight in a sense of wonder, seeing creation as a window onto God; both see imagination as the source of human creativity, the divine at work within us and all about us, in whose light we see light. Both Celtic and Ignatian spirituality delight in the extraordinariness of the ordinary and see the spiritual in the material and the material as the spiritual seen from without. Both spiritualities are Christ-centred, the risen Christ, present in every detail of creation, in the life and joy of the world and in the tears of things.

This short book, clearly and beautifully written, both lifts the heart and enlightens the mind. It presents a way of seeing the world as God's cloak – a sign, and an effective sign, of God's presence. Changing our perception, it changes the way we relate to the world, leading us to a sense of wonder and reverence for the world and for one another. The resources for this spirituality are all around us: we have access to it with all our senses, with every breath we breathe and through our wonderful gift of imagination. Every bush is burning for those with eyes to see, because God is in all things and all things are in God.

GERARD W. HUGHES, SJ

Preface

Creation has ever been my place of resurrection! In it I have found inspiration, peace and sometimes healing. And deeper than that, I have glimpsed the image of the creator, imprinted upon the fabric like a watermark on a banknote.

Certain words will recur repeatedly in the text, words like wonder and mystery, imagination and creativity. That is because they express my own sense of creation. Wonder is a product of the contemplation of nature, stemming from an awareness of the mystery of things. Mystery is the unfathomed, unfathomable depth of being. Our own participation in being gives us that restlessness that is so obvious in modern life, ever seeking further, deeper, until we come to rest, as Augustine says, in the source of mystery which is God.

I have used two early sources of spirituality to embellish the text, sources which, though early, have nevertheless proved themselves to be rich wells for a spirituality which is relevant to our world, namely Celtic and Ignatian. The early Celtic Christians of the seventh to ninth centuries found a rich source of inspiration in nature, as their ancestors had before them. My own Celtic blood has responded to that. Ignatius of Loyola, in the fifteenth century, left to his Jesuit followers, and through them to numerous Christians, a seam of spiritual gold which we still mine today, and in which I as a Jesuit have been nurtured.

These two sources provide useful examples for the text, but also give to a modern outlook the sort of root in tradition that all Christianity aspires to. God, after all, does not change his address.

To experience wonder and encounter mystery we need look no further, initially, than the human body–soul complex. In this book body and soul stand as symbols for those old dualities, matter–spirit, earth–heaven, which we are perpetually tempted to place against each other as though they were enemies, thus destroying wholeness and unity in creation. My hope is to bring them together more strongly, uniting them in Christ.

Two other sources will be obvious in the text: Teilhard de Chardin, the Jesuit palaeontologist whose love of created matter and spirit was a consuming interest in his life and guided his work. His influence will be apparent, though I have quoted scarcely any of his actual words. The other source of inspiration is poetry of various kinds, especially that of another Jesuit lover of nature, Gerard Manley Hopkins.

The theme of matter and spirit in creation will be approached through different avenues, and this will cause a good deal of overlap in the material. Repetition is an Ignatian precept!

Early in each chapter I have noted a few points that will be covered in that chapter. Each chapter ends with a 'reprise', bearing upon the material dealt with in that section. Some suggestions will appear in the text for prayer or reflection or simply for appreciating the wonder and mystery of creation.

May God find joy in what he has created!

1
The Mystery of Matter
Matter–spirit and imagination

I start this book from where I stand, on the earth. We are children of the earth, says no less a theologian than Karl Rahner, caught up as we are in birth and death and living in a body dependent on air, food and the movements that maintain us. The earth is our home and our environment. So I begin my wanderings by considering the stuff of the earth: matter.

Matter!? I hear you cry. Surely we live in too materialistic a society as it is? Aren't we simply up to the neck in matter and total materialism? We need to hear less of matter and more of spirit, more of soul. Materialism has taken us over and killed spiritual values. Were we not even told, in the latter half of the twentieth century, that God, the Ultimate Spirit, was dead?

Indeed it is true that we live in a materialistic time. Matter and spirit must act together.

Our materialist society

Turning the pages of a colour magazine such as many newspapers produce at the weekend (one of six or seven items! – the single newspaper of yore spawned several off-spring: Sport, Travel, Gardening, Colour Supplement, etc., etc.), I found myself speculating on our materialist society.

What did I find there? Many pages were devoted to fashion; there was a lot about health, pop idols and TV. Filmstars were rampant, and of course, the makers of money were flagged up as makers of happiness. Sex is paraded as the indispensable commodity. Everyone wants to be happy, and the way to it is advertised, in the magazine, as money, beauty, power, popularity and influence. Failing all these, alcohol and drugs can be found down a side-alley.

Science has gradually ousted mystery. We are immersed in a society whose aims and preoccupations are material benefit: holidays, house, car, money, food, TV, etc. It is the materialistic dream: improved material means happiness. And yet, so often, the desired result – happiness – is not forth-coming. Science has produced the material improvement, but not the happiness. Still materialists decry spirit, and spirit fanatics denounce matter. Both matter and spirit are part of creation. So, in this chapter we turn our attention to

1 Matter and mystery, the mystery of matter.
2 Body and spirit as components of the human make-up and both important.
3 Imagination as the way into the invisible world of spirit.
4 Creativity as part of the image of God in us.

Matter

You may ask, Why should it be necessary to consider so obvious a thing? The world, you might say, is thoroughly materialistic and needs no encouragement in that sphere, but is ailing for want of spirit. I answer: God made matter and it is imbued with his Spirit. It matters.

To get an intimate sense of matter you cannot do better than work with clay. Get a lump of damp clay and work it with your hands, just for the sensation, the feel, of matter.

Pray while you do it, as you express what is in you. Don't worry whether it is good art, or figurative. Just express what is in you.

Teilhard de Chardin

Let me put two scenes before you, concerning a child called Pierre Teilhard de Chardin, who was born at Sarcenat in the Massif Central in France:

Scene 1: The boy is wandering about in the back yard of his home and comes across an old bit of farm machinery – a piece of iron. He picks it up, and begins to turn it over in his hand.

He loves the feel of it, the solidity and hardness. There is something permanent about it that appeals to him. He puts it down where he found it, realizing it is too bulky and dirty to carry into the house, where he would have to answer the awkward question: 'What are you doing with that dirty piece of iron, Pierre? Throw it away!' So he conceals it where he found it, and comes back, time and time again, to the corner of the yard where he left it, making a sort of pilgrimage to see it and touch it.

As time goes on he collects pieces of iron, the head of a bolt, bits of old machines. They are all thick, hard, heavy and tough. It is the durability that appeals to him. However, as he grows older it satisfies him less, because he realizes that it is man-made, it rusts, becomes pitted, less permanent than he hoped. He desired something more constitutive of the fabric of the world.

Scene 2: The child has grown and wanders further. He stands staring up at the great rock-face rearing up into the sky above him. His eyes glint in awe. He moves closer to the rock, slowly, as though approaching a Deity. Reaching out the flat of his hand he places it on the surface, feeling the texture of the stone with reverence. Here was what he desired. Solid, permanent. The very stuff of the world. Rock.

Eventually, reluctantly, with glances backwards, he moves on.

Prayer on a rock

Find a piece of rock, as large as is convenient for you to handle. Spend time with it in your hands, sensing the texture, the smoothness or roughness, feeling the weight of it, the solidity. Pray with it in your hands, thanking God for the gift of rock. Pray with a line or two from Psalm 18:

> I love you Yahweh, my strength . . .
> Yahweh is my rock, and my bastion,
> my deliverer is my God.
> I take shelter in him, my rock . . .
>
> Who else is God but Yahweh,
> who else a rock save our God?

Geologist

Moving on, as the years went by, Teilhard began to collect stones. His love for the matter of the earth grew as he observed and collected. Solidity. As child and boy he knew he needed solidity, permanence. Metal was manufactured, whereas rock is the stuff of the earth, the root or matrix of being. He became a geologist, and then a palaeontologist with a worldwide reputation. How he would have been riveted, as I was, by the sights on television of the eruption of the volcano that overwhelmed the town of Goma in the

Congo. To be able to see, as we did, the inner power of matter, a seething sea of molten rock, goaded by the heat of immense fires bursting the skin of the earth and showering and pouring down the mountain, devastating everything in its way . . . a truly awe-inspiring sight.

'Hymn to Matter'

It was the sense of wonder and awe that was being stirred in his soul when he contemplated matter. In fact, he wanted to be immersed in an ocean of it. He wrote a 'Hymn to Matter': 'Son of Earth, steep yourself in the sea of Matter!' This might give an impression of someone having a delicious swim in a blue Caribbean sea! But the hymn takes in the harshness and impenetrability of matter as much as its softness and fertility. He sees it as mighty and untamable like the magma at Goma, as well as its calm beauty. It uproots us and moves us on, wounds us and dresses our wounds. He blesses matter.

For me, Teilhard is of particular interest. Though I am no geologist, I love rock. We share a common interest in created nature. We share a common thread in our roots, in that a large part of my background is Celtic, and he was a Celt from France. But there is another significant factor shared in common, and that is that he also became a Jesuit, a follower of Ignatius of Loyola. So, for me, he constitutes a remarkable link-point between the Celtic world and the spirituality of Ignatius. And for both of them, matter and spirit interact and are one.

The matter–spirit union

Spirit is matter seen from within; matter is spirit seen from without. Matter and spirit act together as one thing. Matter participates in God's self-manifestation. Mind does not exist without a body, as music must have an instrument. So matter participates in the spiritual.

The attitude implicit in my upbringing (by education and religion) was of a fundamental difference, even opposition, between matter and spirit, body and soul – two substances, different in nature, two species of being.

In starting this book with this consideration of the importance of matter, I simply want to underline an attitude to created things which is different from the one I was brought up with. The substance of the earth is not simply a commodity to be used as a resource. Even the human body is in danger of being seen in this way, a cloned resource of spare parts for curing diseases, a sort of biological tool-kit or pack of spare fuses. Once our sense of wonder in the presence of creation is replaced by a pragmatic 'What use is it?' then we lose any hope of transcending the bounds of sense knowledge.

Body and soul

Perhaps the most familiar case of matter and spirit cooperating is in the human being.

> What a piece of work is man!
> How noble in reason, how infinite in faculties.
> In form and moving, how express and admirable.
> In action how like an angel,
> In apprehension how like a god!
> The beauty of the world, the paragon of animals.

So the Bard tells us. And yet, he says, the human being is the 'quintessence of dust'!

Quintessence of dust is a good description of what God

produced when he created human beings, as in the Book of Genesis. God took the dust of the earth and breathed into it the breath of the Spirit. Body and soul. Francis Thompson in the poem 'Any saint' talks of the human being as a swinging-wicket set between the unseen and seen.

The Bible does not know any great separation between body and soul, but succeeding centuries have not dealt kindly with the human being. There has been a tendency in the history of society to swing to one pole or the other. The body has been emphasized to the detriment of spirit, or spirit to the denigration of the body. The materialists did away with the soul some time ago, though they haven't quite managed to kill it off. On the other hand, religious traditions can be accused of going in the opposite direction, concentrating on the spiritual in such a way as to oppose it to the corporeal. The attempt has been, on the one hand to explain all facets of human life in terms of matter only, bodily functions which can be mapped, interfered with and imitated in purely material terms; and on the other, to assume that the body is but an obstacle to spiritual activity and purity and the sooner shaken off the better.

The challenge is always to recognize both sides of the remarkable thing called the human being and do justice to both. What is a body without breath!

Body awareness

Spend a time simply being aware of your body. Sit on an upright chair, your back straight, your feet comfortably on the ground, like a statue of one of the Kings on the Nile. Let your hands rest loosely in your lap. Let your awareness sink down inside your body, like water sinking into the earth. Become aware of your feet resting on the ground, not *thinking* of them, but aware of them touching the ground.

Then slowly, with total attention, become aware of each part of your legs, working upwards, past knees and thighs into your midriff. As you go, be aware of any tension and relax it. Attention is the key. If you are attending totally to your body you will not be thinking. When you find your attention straying, when you find that you are thinking, just turn your attention back into your body. In this way, work your way right up through your body and down again. At the end, thank God for your body.

Creativity and matter

God created matter and spirit, not just one of them. When he looked at what he had created and 'saw that it was good', he was not just admiring his invention of hordes of spirits. He was looking at the cosmos, the stars, the sky, the waters, the land, the rocks and soil, the plants, the animals.

Born into this world of things, of matter and spirit, we find God in it, in and through it. We do not oscillate from body to spirit and back, but act as one being who is enfleshed spirit. To confine ourselves to one or other is to restrict the life that God has given to us, and which is his life in us. We are likely to die of thirst, or hunger, since our needs are those of a body–spirit.

Matter, as well as spirit, is the residing place of God's creativity. Eckhart, the German mystic, says, 'We inherit the tremendous creative power of God.' The creativity of the human race has been obvious throughout our history. In fact, it has gone beyond itself in the twentieth century when the human race has seen itself playing with forces beyond its control. We now have the capability of destroying the whole race, of reaching the stars and of reconstructing our bodies and modifying life itself.

There is every reason to believe, then, that one of the

most godlike traits that we have inherited is that of creativity. Imagination and creativity are intimately linked. The imagination is a proper place to find God. We need to grow more and more into this likeness; like God, we need to create. Yet this is not a sphere which has ever been acknowledged by the Church as more than an adjunct. Beethoven, Michelangelo were never in line for beatification, even though their creativity was truly godlike and a blessing on the world. Artists are deeply in contact with the beauty of the creation, a sacramental contact.

God is love. Love and beauty walk together, hand in hand. We talk of 'making love' as a reference to the sexual activity that gives rise to life. It is the creative action producing being. In this, the creative activity of God is at work through us, and in expressing that creativity we are acting out the image of God in us. In the risen Christ the activity of God is at work to perfection. Death, the great separation, is overcome. New life is pronounced.

Think of the painter or sculptor in training, spending long hours staring at a still life, or a model, drawing and copying from life. He or she is trained to 'see', to observe the material world, and to produce on canvas or in clay what is seen. Yet, if the painter or sculptor goes no further than making an exact copy of the object, then the artist's function has already been usurped by the photographer. Frances Wickes, in *The Inner World of Choice*, states that a work of art is not just an imitation of the object because the spirit in the artist is always shaping and reshaping, and transforming in a world of eternal meanings.

Material is perhaps the more immediate reality, and through it the world of spirit, of 'eternal meanings' as Wickes puts it, is seen and expressed. This way of entering in by matter, and finding spiritual reality, is often called 'sacramental'. Our friend Teilhard saw everything interconnected, holistic, all-embracing, unifying. Studying the 'without' of things (outward appearance) he was led to discover their 'within'. Matter and spirit are not two separate things but aspects of the same reality, one leading to the other. Matter discloses spirit. So he praised the spiritual power of matter, as a flood of energy, the crucible of spirit.

Temptation of matter

It is an unfortunate fact that many of us have been brought up more conscious of the 'temptation' of matter than its strength and content, and spiritual blessing. We are more inclined to consider the body a hindrance to holiness than a blessing given us to enable us to love and reverence God, creation and one another. We are part of God's creative action, communing with God through the earth and life, embodied spirit with a reverence for matter.

The temptation to dualism

The Russian mystic Solovyev saw two opposing tendencies. On the one hand, glorifying man at the expense of God; and on the other, glorifying God by denigrating the human. Both of these are extremes to be avoided.

There has been a considerable current of religion which has condemned matter as evil, corrupt and to be avoided. It all stemmed from an ancient system that thought of two creators rather than one, a wonderful God who created spirit and who was wholly spiritual; and another Fabricator who made material things. The one was good, the other bad, and therefore their products were good (in the case of spirit and all things spiritual) and bad (in the case of matter and all things material). The result was the separation of matter from spirit, earth from heaven, body from soul. The good God was firmly confined to the spiritual sphere, and as a result, it became possible to reach that God only by renouncing matter and body and earth and all that they contain. For Teilhard there was no such division. Through evolution, matter and spirit were no longer two things, but two states of one thing. And he appeals to us never to think of matter as 'accursed' or 'evil'. He addresses us in those terms, supposing we might think to pursue Spirit in a world of pure thought and angelic freedom from matter. But in trying to do this we are likely to perish of hunger! For we are created body and soul. As body we are made of matter, flesh, veins and blood, nerves, gut and brain. They are not just adjuncts, things we would be better off without, put there to catch us out, or, as some scientists would say, bundles of instincts and appetites and nothing more. For these things have been said by those who saw the body only as an obstacle to the spirit within.

The killing of joy

If you think that all this talk of dualism is exaggerated I would invite you to read the description in the *Carmina Gadelica* of Carmichael of a visit he made to a woman living in Ness at the northern end of the Isle of Lewis in the Outer Hebrides. Religion, he discovered, was a serious business, not to be confused with 'entertainment' and thus even with joy. While her charity lacked nothing in caring for his needs to dry his clothes (after trudging all day through the bog!) and his hunger, she condemned the foolishness of the days of her youth when weddings were celebrated with games and enjoyment.

Surprised at this, Carmichael asked whether they had any music or dancing at their weddings now? To which she replied with great grief and surprise in her tone, 'May the

Possessor keep you! I see that you are a stranger in Lewis, or you would not ask such a question!'

Whereas in the old days each house would have had a pipe or fiddle, when the ministers came these things were condemned and destroyed as perversions. A few years ago a violin player died on the island of Eigg. He was well-known for the brilliance of his playing, the beauty of his tone, and the great variety of the tunes and his variations of them which, of course, died with him. During his life, a preacher denounced him: 'Thou art down there behind the door, thou miserable man with thy grey hair, playing thine old fiddle with the cold hand without and the devil's fire within.' Pressured by his family he sold the violin to a pedlar for ten shillings! It was made by a pupil of Stradivarius and was famous for its sweet tone. 'It was not at all the thing that was got for it that grieved my heart so sorely,' he declared, 'but the parting with it! the parting with it! and that I myself gave the best cow in my father's fold for it when I was young.' His voice faltered and a tear fell. He was never seen to smile again.

That last statement struck me most deeply. 'He was never seen to smile again.' The source of his joy, of his self-expression, of his exercise of the great gift of music that God had given him, had been stifled.

When we forsake matter, and the building-blocks with which God created the universe, we forsake the energy and creativity invested in matter by the creator. Part of that energy is expressed in joy. Thus human play, entertainment, music, and other ways in which we discover and express the goodness of life, are expelled when we abolish these elements. The result is like a plant deprived of water, a shrivelling up of the tissues of the heart and soul.

God's creative imagination

We are God's creation, the result of the creative power, the creative imagination of God. That creativity which produced the whole of the cosmos comes down to us in our own nature, and makes us, too, creative. In a book called *The Artist's Way*, Julia Cameron underlines the importance of creativity to the artist, or rather to the artist in all of us. Life is creative energy which is present in the created world. We ourselves are part of that world and we inherit the gift of creativity from our creator, just as a child will inherit intelligence or artistic temperament from a parent. When we use our creative gift we are singing our own Magnificat, Mary's hymn of praise to God who had used her gift of creativity to give birth to the child Jesus. The image of God in human beings is their creative potential. In Celtic times the artist was given an important place in society. The chief poet was the 'king-maker', the one who named the new king. Why was such an importance attached to people who in our time are regarded as of little significance, and often as eccentric? Why? Because the poets were the ones who could see with the creativity of God and express it. In fact, in early Irish literature, the poets (the *filid*) were reckoned to be 'seers' with mystical wisdom. That wisdom came from God, it was divine wisdom. Drinking the water of the 'well of wisdom' was considered to be a 'sacramental' action.

Imagination

When we consider creativity we are inevitably involved with imagination. It is a wonderful faculty, not present in any comparable way in the rest of the animal kingdom. Animals tend to act out of an instinctual pattern which scarcely varies with repeated use. Human beings, on the other hand, have a freedom and capability of inventing new things out of the rich pool of imagination. Science itself, that bastion of laws discovered and verified by strict experiment, in fact arrives at many of its great discoveries as a result of initial intuition and imagination. It is involved in hope. Madame Curie, stirring the great pot of matter from which she hoped to extract uranium, must in some way have 'seen' the result of her efforts. Imagination provides the spark of insight that enables a scientist to pursue a particular line of research. It is in a way infinite, yet dealing in concrete reality, while not confined to any one form. It is quasi-infinite, sharing qualities of both matter and spirit, a nexus.

A nexus or link, in fact, between body and soul, imagination links the abstraction of idea and the concrete reality of matter.

Imagination is the particular aspect of Spirit that is creative. It opens up the area of possibility, and so enables things to happen. It showed to Ignatius of Loyola the possibility of serving God rather than worldly pursuits.

Day dreams

Ignatius lay on his couch after the shattering of his legs at the Battle of Pamplona, and he dreamed dreams. His imagination floated freely, as we might think was often the case in his early life, imagining himself winning duels with consummate sword-play, and thereby impressing the lady of his dreams so powerfully as to be her instant champion. Unfortunately, it was only a dream, because the lady in question was probably a princess, or at any rate a person far above Ignatius' social class. It didn't stop him from imagining the scenes of his triumphs! His roaming imagination wandered across horizons as wide as the earth, and his spirit was as strong as the Celtic champion Cuchullain, when the battle fervour was on him.

We may feel, at times, that our poor religion has been stripped down to a skeleton of dogmatic proclamations which leave little room for creativity.

Both Ignatius and the Celts were people of wonder and mystery, fed by the lovely gift of imagination. This quality is what makes them particularly apt models for our spirituality today. From looking at them we might glean helpful inspiration for ourselves, particularly in terms of prayer and worship. The really memorable days are those in which our imagination has achieved expression. Keats talks of the 'truth' of imagination, the truth of the beauty seen by imagination.

Pure imagination?

How often were we told as children, 'That is pure imagination!' or, 'You're just imagining it' (and therefore it is not real!). Perhaps this is why imagination is not trusted by institutions – it is too free, moving easily through all the regions of knowledge. It dances out beyond the walls of rules and customs, and so does not easily conform to rigid confinements. The cage of the law tries to imprison the spirit, while imagination breaks free: theologians are not supposed to be imaginative but to remain hemmed into the guidelines; when they do move out they fall foul of the institution. Perhaps that is why the early Celtic Church fared so ill within the wider Church.

Obviously, imagination can lead us down the garden path, and serve evil instead of good, as indeed can the intellect. Many a tyrant, pervert and torturer has been a person of lurid imagination. It gave rise to the strange vision in Ignatius' time at Manresa, a creature with bright eyes that captivated him until he realized it was a symbol of temptation. This simply illustrates what a power it has to lead and move us. It can be the proper leader of all human enterprises;

but it has to keep in touch with the world of observation. The fact that imagination, a powerful tool, can lead in dangerous directions does not invalidate its use any more than the wrong use of intellect invalidates *its* use. Indeed, should we criticize God for inventing beings that were to become devils?

In the image of God

One writer, George MacDonald, in *Defence of Imagination*, goes so far as to see the likeness of human beings to God, not in the intellect or will, but in the imagination as the power giving form and embodiment to thought and aspiration. The human being *bodies forth* God's thinking since creation is the direct result of the divine imagination. Yet we proceed both from the love of God and from his imagination.

The Spirit is the Go-Between God (see the book of that name by J. V. Taylor) who establishes connections in our lives between each other and between ourselves and the environment and, through these, between ourselves and God. The Spirit is at the root of the sense of wonder and imagination.

Harking back and harking forth

Test your faculty of imagination in two ways: as imaginative memory, and as a view of the future. Remember a scene from earlier in your life, a scene that you remember with joy, a place, an event, a person. Enter into that scene again, relive it in your imagination. Feel again what you felt then.

Now imagine a scene as if from a future time, and live in that fully. Sense the power of the imagination, and its motive force.

Celtic sundance

When the Celts saw the sun 'dancing' and angels present, was this imagination? Certainly, but it was also an expression of religious belief.

Getting stuck = lack of imagination

This chapter has reminded us of the benefits of imaginative creativity in our spiritual lives. The two traditions we have been appealing to were particularly strong in this. The creativity of the Celts and Ignatius gave rise to a dynamic faith filled with awe, determination, energy and sheer delight. These are attributes which do not strike us as redolent of our churches today, in many cases. We have tended to become bogged down in our worship and in our lives in general. Getting stuck is a function of routine and lack of imagination. Any relationship in life tends to get stuck after a while and needs to be worked at if it is to survive and thrive. We can find great inspiration and imagination in both the Celtic and Ignatian traditions. In the exercise of imagination in prayer we become more aware of the presence of God, more able to see deeper into the wonders of creation.

Can we not regain something
of that Celtic quality of heart,
the excitement, the love that gave them eyes
to see the image of the soul, and the spirit of a place?
That Other World was very real to them, a place
of which our space is but a shadow.
Wonder was no rare quality of mind
but the heart's reaction to the world about.
They saw, they wondered and emblazoned
on the Gospel page, the faith and art we marvel at today.
And he, the Knight from Quipcuzcoa
was galvanized by sheer imagination
to a gallantry that pierces still through time.
Why is our God mundane to us, so routine
that we profess a boredom in his presence?
The spark in us has been blown out. And yet,
if we but wish to feel the bound of love
we have to enter into that great world
imagination weaves within our hearts.

2
Transparent Creation
A window to God

> The world is charged with the grandeur of God
> It will flame out, like shining from shook foil;
> It gathers to a greatness like the ooze of oil
> Crushed.
>
> ('God's Grandeur')

So wrote the poet Hopkins, with his keen perception of the presence of God in all created things. It is that sense of creation as a 'window' onto God that we pay special attention to in this chapter. But we have, as a race, put so much dirt on the window that we have made it much harder to see through to the creator.

1 Through creation, our environment, we glimpse the creator and some of his attributes.
2 Our exploitation of the environment is destroying it. There is a responsibility for us to replace greed with respect and care.
3 We need to be still, receptive, open to wonder and mystery to do this.

Environment: window to God or rubbish dump?

A lad walked towards me in Sauchiehall Street in Glasgow, swallowing the dregs of a can of Irn Bru. Without even a sideways glance he tossed the empty can into the recess of a shop door where it joined two other cans, a carton and the remains of a take-away. The nearby rubbish bin goes unacknowledged. The same street the morning after a public holiday looks like the aftermath of a battle between beer cans and Kentucky fried chicken (remains of). Dead cans, food, cartons are strewed over the whole area. The street itself has turned into a rubbish dump. This chapter is concerned with creation, that is, with everything created, the wonder and mystery of it. So why do I start out by considering it as a rubbish dump?

Environment is an alive topic today. Political parties have to pay lip service to it if nothing more, because they realize that it really is an issue. Accounts of the ways in which humankind are gradually destroying their own world make unhappy reading. They paint a depressing picture of punctured ozone layers, animals dying out, seabirds stiff with oil, foodstuffs sprayed with DDT, soil poisoned to its depths, water lethal to drink, rainforests chopped down, radioactive seaside resorts and the atmosphere itself becoming poisoned, to mention but a few. This picture is played across the screens of our televisions and our minds daily. And green men and women climb over fences and onto ships to proclaim the evils of our neglect of the environment.

Isaiah proclaimed something similar in his time:

> Ravaged, ravaged the earth,
> despoiled, despoiled.
> The earth is mourning, withering,
> The world is pining, withering,
> the heavens are pining away with the earth.
> The earth is defiled under its inhabitants' feet
> for they have transgressed the law . . .
>
> (Isaiah 24)

The reason for all this is not far to seek: human greed. National economy is placed before cleaning up pollution in importance, and so we go on exploiting the earth, and pouring rubbish into the atmosphere. It is, of course, a disastrously short-sighted policy which will rebound on us in the end.

Green issues, then, are alive and humming down the wire. Our concern stems from two sources: first of all, the fear that we are destroying the very earth and atmosphere that supports us, fouling our own nest, sickening ourselves; and then, that we are destroying something that in our enlightened moments we know to be inherently good and, at best, beautiful.

The trouble is that few people feel a responsibility for the state of affairs. We worry about our little shopping list of sins, swearing, forgetting our night prayers, being unkind and a host of other trivialities. Polluting the atmosphere does not seem to enter into it.

John and smoke

Imagine a man, let's call him John, pleasantly middle-aged (fighting off the spread by jogging) and affably middle-class (without noticeable prejudice), reasonably well off and working for a drugs firm. He goes on retreat to bolster his prayer-life rather than be aware of his sinfulness. One morning he goes out into the field at the back of the retreat house to jog before breakfast. The sun is rising above the pylons and casting a rich shaft of light across the field. He feels its warmth as he runs (slowly) past holly bushes, and a confusion of weeds. He feels healthy and full of life. No sign of sin.

Suddenly, a chill strikes him. He looks up to see that the sun's light has been obscured by a large swathe of smoke. He stops in dismay, since there had been no cloud in the sky, and he searches for the source of it. It is emanating in great voluminous folds from three factory chimneys in the distance. Even as he stands there the sun is blotted out, and a species of night descends on the countryside. 'Damn pollution!' he mutters. 'Why don't they do something about it!?' They. It is always the other who is doing the evil deed! But as he continued to jog round the field a memory was stirred in his mind. John had asked a doctor to come into the factory where he worked as a manager to check the health of the staff and the conditions under which they worked. The doctor had reported back to him that the working conditions were reasonable and the personnel in good shape. 'It's the people in the neighbourhood of the factory that suffer!' Why? Because of the amount of poison the drugs firm was pouring into the ground and into the river nearby. He gave facts and figures to prove that the occurrence of cancer in the area round the factory was 20 per cent higher than the national average, and supplied an analysis of the toxicity of the chemical wastes. John had not had time to think about the doctor's report at the time, and it had got wedged into a pile of papers on his desk. Only now, at the retreat house, where he had time and space to ponder on these things, had that report come back into his mind. Suddenly, like an arrow finding the joint in a suit of armour, a sense of his own part in this, a sense of his sin, had penetrated him.

He realized it was not just 'them' causing the ravaging of the earth, but he himself was involved. A new awareness began to grow in him, a stark sense of responsibility as part of the human race, for the desecration of creation. Facts and figures which he knew already, but had kept in the cellar of his mind, came flooding in, the pollution caused by humankind, Chief Seattle's letter (whether genuine or not did not now matter!), the laying waste of the rainforests, and a host of other examples. From there it spread to an awareness of the causes of all this, the oppression and injustice and greed that seems to be written into the human story.

No doubt he would experience the helplessness of being only a small part of all that, not directly responsible, yet caught up in a web of responsibility. Perhaps that is why it is difficult to experience it as sin – our shopping list, we feel, is more under our control!

Reversing the tide: awareness

To reverse the tide of pollution and devastation of the planet would seem to be a task too monumental for our fragile minds to grasp. 'What can we/I do about it?' we ask. Perhaps all we can do initially is become aware of the problem, and aware of the sinfulness involved in it. Awareness can, in the end, change attitudes. Aware, too, in another sense, of nature and the environment.

To experience nature immediately is the most beneficial form of prayer and reflection on creation. Walk or sit somewhere in woods or fields or garden, just being aware of what you see, like a gold-prospector gazing at a pan of grit from the river, looking for specks of gold. Stop long with a leaf or a piece of bark, just appreciating texture and design and colour. Don't hurry. The voice of nature is often quiet and shy. Use, as far as possible, all of your senses, eyes for colour and design, touch for texture, ears for the sounds around you, smell for the cut grass or the woodbine, and even taste (with care!). Give God praise and thanks. Remember to be still. When you are with your lover you want to be alone. Being alone in landscape is a way of communing with it, and entering into its mystery. Our relationship to it is reciprocal. Our courtesy towards the earth will enter the relationships in our lives. So I will find in others the dignity, the wisdom, the mystery that I find in the landscape.

What are you seeking?

What is to be gained by encouraging this sense of God present in the earth and all elements?

For the spiritual person it is, of course, an expression of a reality which cannot be seen, but is nevertheless real. The person standing in the sunshine on a glorious summer day (as in 'Hebridean altars'), feels the need to praise the sun-blessed day as a jewel dropped from God's hand. What a wonderful, beautiful mind this day must come from, he says, and asks that this loveliness pass into his spirit, and flow out from there in the right-doing of his life, and the love which gives itself. God's Spirit is within us, and we can have reference to the Spirit to guide us.

God's creative action

Creation is, as we are aware from the Book of Genesis in the Bible, the product of God's creativity, the product, we might say, of the imagination of God. He created 'out of nothing, by his word' as the old catechism used to say. Some would depict God's creativity as playfulness.

All creation, therefore, is dependent on God, has a participation in the *energeia* of God. Everything participates in him. There is not one thing that exists which did not come through God's power. Evolution itself is God's creative act. Meditate on Psalms 8 and 104, which are creation psalms. Use the method called 'Lectio divina', a simple way of reading until a phrase or sentence catches your attention, and stopping with that, repeat it over and over to let it sink in. Talk to God from all that comes to mind from the phrase. Give praise and thanks. Don't hurry on, but stay quietly with whatever has come to you. Then move back to the text to the next significant phrase.

Go into the park and sit on a bench, or on the grass, and be aware of the air, of any odours borne on the air. Watch a bird that you would not normally spend time looking at, a hedge sparrow, or a pigeon, and pay special attention to it. The Jesuit poet Gerard Manley Hopkins made many notes, both in words and in simple drawings, of trees and twigs and flowers. Try doing this, just for your own perusal, with great simplicity. To draw on a scrap of paper part of the branch of a tree makes you look, observe, everything about it.

God is beyond

A word of caution needs to be inserted here. Nature may be our way to see God, but it is only an inkling, only partial. The mystery of God's being is way beyond our perception and not knowable by us in itself. Our knowledge of him, if I may be permitted a crude comparison, is a bit like that of the optimist who, to test the strength of his optimism, was given a Christmas present of a pile of horse dung. He was discovered sitting by it with a grin on his face saying, 'Where there is so much dung there just *must* be a pony!'

Where there is evidence there just must be a creator. But the knowledge we get of the creator from the evidence is tiny. The optimist did not, after all, know much of the pony from the pile of dung!

God is not knowable in his own being. Our own knowledge of his creation is an inkling we get, but it can be only partial. Science has reckoned it can know phenomenal reality – but that can never be exhaustive.

Celtic and Ignatian

When it comes to a consideration of the sacredness of nature, our two traditions, Celtic and Ignatian, are very pertinent.

When asked why Celtic spirituality is so popular today many people would say, 'because it is rooted in nature', in fact 'green' in the modern sense. The picture we are often presented with is of the Celtic saint at one with his or her environment, observant and respectful of nature. The same claim would probably not be made immediately for St Ignatius. Few would automatically think of him as a nature-lover, wandering the woods reciting poetry and describing twigs in the manner of a Gerard Manley Hopkins. Yet the man who contemplated with inspiration the stars at night on the roof of the house in Rome where he was staying and wrote down the 'Contemplation for love' is surely a visionary who could see God's eyes shining through the fabric of the world. Where God is recognized to be present there is a call for reverence and respect.

Saints and animals

The companionship of the saints with animals is a strange aspect of their relationship with nature. Columbanus with the beasts and birds gathered meekly round him could be a scene lifted from *The House at Pooh Corner*! Is the pet squirrel poking its head out of his cloak trying to tell us something? Even the pragmatic Ignatius trusted the wisdom of animals. Riding from Manresa on a mule he entered into an argument with a Moor about Our Lady. After the Moor had gone on Ignatius felt he had not taken sufficiently punitive action to protect the honour of Our Lady. His aggressive instinct to pursue the Moor to a nearby village and there deal with him was countered by a surge of new-found grace, telling him this might not be the way to deal with the problem. So he decided to let the mule find the way to go. Mule-sense led the beast away from the village and the conflict. Perhaps there is a wisdom in nature which has been suppressed in human beings.

More Celtic pets

There are Celtic tales of hermits being led to the potential sites of their cells by dumb animals – though this is not so dumb when you realize that they would instinctively know where there was water! The animals were sometimes set to look after each other and regard each other as brothers and sisters. As when a fox reverted to type and took the boss's shoes off to his former den to eat! In our day this would certainly end with the shooting of the fox or hunting of it; but St Ciaran sent Badger to bring him back to heel, which he did. Mo Chua, a hermit, harboured three creatures, a cock, a mouse and a fly – an unlikely series of pets in any household. The cock crowed him awake for matins at midnight, the mouse nibbled his ear to wake him in the morning and the fly acted as a sort of live bookmark by running along the line Mo was reading and then remaining, like a cursor, at the place he stopped.

St Kevin of Glendalough, praying in a chapel scarcely bigger than himself, had to stick his arms out the windows in order to pray in the accustomed manner. A blackbird made a nest in his hand so he had to remain there until the eggs were hatched!

Quaint tales? Yes, but they underline a basic relationship of the human being to nature, and the animals among themselves, reminiscent of the lion lying down with the lamb in Isaiah – a foretaste of redeemed nature (Romans 8) or harking back to the garden of Eden. The human being is part of created nature, not set apart from it. The juxtaposition of unlikely bedfellows is a statement that God's ways are not ours.

Children of the earth

As part of creation, human beings cannot claim the sort of superiority over it that enables them to use nature as a convenience and resource. Our roots are in the soil since God took the dust of the earth to fashion us.

The early Celts were 'green' only in the sense that they acknowledged themselves as part of nature. They respected creation as they respected their own selves. Nature is our environment, we are part of it. Rooted in it. There is a picture, a self-portrait, of the Mexican painter Frida Kahlo, which represents her lying on the ground with roots emanating from her body into the soil. It was her way of depicting our connection with the earth, our being part of the earth. When we lose our connection with the soil of our begetting we lose perspective.

God of the everyday

Celtic spirituality recognized God present in the activity of everyday life. The blessing used by a woman going to collect the hen's eggs (given in the *Carmina Gadelica* of Carmichael) and the explanation of it by Noel O'Donoghue are an intriguing example of this. The woman, placing her hand on her breast, associates her own motherhood with that of the hen, moving to the nest 'sunwise' so as to evoke the power of the sun. In this way, she makes of an everyday action a religious rite within the sacredness of creation.

Respect for the earth

Reverence for the earth as sacred was not confined to the Celts, being common to the native Indians of America and the Aboriginal natives of Australia to name but two. For cultures such as these, sacred and secular came together. The sacred gives rise to the element of mystery and hence of wonder in our awareness.

I look out of my window on a visit to the island of Skye at the rock faces of the Quiraing, a wall of basalt hiding a strange landscape. I desire to investigate as Moses was drawn to the burning bush. Landscape often harbours mystery, and my desire was an expression of the quest for the depths, for what is beyond. Landscapes, says Barry Lopez, are crucibles of mystery, containing a deep sense of the infinite. It is not improved by our technology, like a JCB pushing God gradually into a ditch!

The Celts loved mystery. It gave their life a richness, a meaning and direction. Mystery implies something further to explore and discover, giving rise to the desire to enter where the mystery resides.

It was a sense of ambiguity allowed for in mystery which the Celts admired, rather than the crystal clear logic and dogmatism of the Romans. There being no monolithic answers they searched for truth in the questions rather than the answers. 'Both–and' rather than 'either–or' was their style. The riddle was more popular with them than the theorem.

Respect for a Lord of creation

A poem which seems to me to capture an attitude of respect and wonder for a part of nature is D. H. Lawrence's poem, 'Snake'.

> A snake came to my water-trough
> On a hot, hot day, and I in pyjamas for the heat,
> To drink there.

His sense of being 'upstaged' by a mere snake was replaced by fear and fascination as the snake 'sipped with his straight mouth'. But the fear began to dominate. His school learning whispered to him that this beast was dangerous and should be killed. Only his fear, he told himself, made him hesitate. But it was not just his fear: he realized that he actually liked his guest, and he declares, humbly, how honoured he felt!

For a moment the voice of his education dominated, driving him, as the snake prepared to depart, to pick up a stick and throw it at the departing reptile, which then withdrew into the hole in the wall with undignified haste.

Immediately he regretted his vulgar act, despising the voice of his accursed education. For the snake had seemed to him like a king of nature:

> And so, I missed my chance with one of the lords
> Of life.
> And I have something to expiate;
> A pettiness.

'Snake' encapsulates both our instinctive and learned reactions to a part of the animal kingdom. To pat the dog and stroke the cat are certainly expressions of our love of creatures, but the attitude that breeds real respect for creation goes further than our instinctive attractions and revulsions. Lawrence found himself fearful in the presence of a poisonous snake, and somehow insulted that this dumb creature could upstage him at the well. His reaction, backed up by his education ('This beast is venomous!') taught him that danger in the natural arena must be eradicated without regard to its inherent value. His enforced stillness before this 'king', his sense of awe and amazement, produced in him that respect which was not yet sufficient to overcome his instinctive and 'educated' reaction which resulted in the flinging of the log at the snake. But beneath the aggression there lay a deep respect which surfaced in his regret for the vulgar, mean and paltry action. In effect, a new kind of education. The sense of wonder and of awe are necessary concomitants of respect.

Nature as a mirror of God

Creation naturally mirrors the attributes of God, such that if we are attentive and willing to contemplate we can find such things there as *Beauty, Abundance, Wildness, Power, Labour, Love, Healing.*

Beauty

The beauty of nature has been sung by poets and musicians for centuries.

> Nothing is so beautiful as Spring, –
> when weeds in wheels grow long and lovely and lush;
> Thrush's eggs look little low heavens, and thrush
> Through the echoing timber does so rinse and wring
> The ear, it strikes like lightnings to hear him sing; . . .
>
> What is all this juice and all this joy?
> A strain of the earth's sweet being in the beginning
> In Eden garden.
>
> (Hopkins, 'Spring')

This sensibility of the beauty of nature gave Celtic spirituality an optimism about nature opposed to the pessimistic tendency of Augustine and the tradition he started.

Abundance

The psalmist sings about the sheer exuberant fullness of

God's provision for the earth. God doesn't do things by halves! In Psalm 65 we read

> You crown the year with your bounty,
> abundance flows in your path,
> the desert pastures overflow,
> the hillsides are filled with joy,
> the meadows are covered with flocks,
> the valleys are clothed in wheat.
> What shouts of joy, what singing!

Any biologist can tell you that of the millions of seeds, eggs, sperm produced by animals or plants, a minute proportion come to fruition, or survive to fertilize or be fertilized. The wonderful television series *The Blue Planet* gave ample testimony to this profligacy of God. Examples in Britain are not so obvious (what about midges in Scotland!) but I can remember driving over the Runcorn Bridge in autumn and being so distracted by the thousands of starlings settling on the struts of the bridge that I nearly drove over the edge.

Wildness

Why do people go seeking wilderness? There is something in our nature that wants the wildness of untouched nature. Over the years of wandering in the hills of the Lake District, and Snowdonia and then in the highlands of Scotland, I have come to a realization that I actually *like* desolate wastes, miles of moorland, slabs of rock. That is why I found myself reacting against the Advent reading from Isaiah:

> A voice cries, 'Make a way for Yahweh in the
> wilderness.
> Lay out a straight highway for our God across
> the desert.

Let every valley be filled in,
and every mountain, every hill be laid flat,
let every cliff become flat ground,
and the ridges become a valley . . .'

(Isaiah 40.3)

I don't want the valleys to be filled in, and the mountains to be brought down and the ridges to be flattened! I love them as they are. The process described there is rather like what happens when a motorway is built. Devastation!

I know the text is meant symbolically, referring to our inner disposition, but my reaction showed me something of my own feelings towards wild land. Much more to my liking is Hopkins' poem about Inversnaid on the banks of Loch Lomond (but situated in a part beyond main roads and easy access). Hopkins' individual use of language adds something to the mystery of a stream cascading down the side of the mountains into the loch. I noticed when typing the poem that the computer's spell-check underlined eight different words even though they had not been misspelled! Here are the first and last verses:

This darksome burn, horseback brown,
His rollrock highroad roaring down,
In coop and in comb the fleece of his foam
Flutes and low to the lake falls home.

What would the world be, once bereft
Of wet and of wildness? Let them be left,
O let them be left, wildness and wet;
Long live the weeds and the wilderness yet.

(Hopkins, 'Inversnaid')

There is a quality in wilderness that corresponds to the desire for freedom within us. The sense of mystery needs nourishment. Being still in a bleak and arid landscape can provide that. The very sparseness of the outer landscape forces the viewer inwards.

What appears at first to be just 'miles and miles of damn all' actually, given time, opens into contemplation and mystery. Ignatius of Loyola used to pray on the roof of the house in Rome where he was staying, contemplating the stars, because, he said, it made him want to serve Our Lord! At one and the same time great space serves to make us 'feel small' and yet expands our soul's desires.

Power

That sense of space opening onto mystery can also be felt in the face of the 'power' of nature. We can be confronted by this power in a number of ways, by a great waterfall, or huge cliffs, or mighty waves in the sea. I felt something of it when I saw the pictures on television of the volcano at Goma, the sight of the flowing lava, the gases, the vents and crevasses looking down into the red-hot bowels of the earth.

The Celtic mind and heart did not care for being squeezed into narrow definitions! St Patrick refers to Christ as the 'True Sun' which allows of a metaphorical use for the brightness and warmth of Christ's presence to us. But it is more than just a metaphor, as is seen from his terrible dream of Satan like a huge rock falling on him and completely paralysing him. Suddenly, he didn't know how or why, he was calling out loud, 'Helias! Helias!' Most people suppose he was calling on Elias. But, as Noel O'Donoghue explains in *An Introduction to Celtic Christianity*, it is far more likely that he was calling out to the Sun! As he was shouting 'Helias' ('Helios' in Greek means 'Sun') he saw the sun rising and its power fell on him and freed him from the rock on top of him. And Patrick then declares that he believed that Christ in his Spirit was helping him.

Patrick was calling out to the sun, and not just as a symbol or metaphor of God's power but the medium through which God comes to us, giving heat and life and light.

Power in creation

Creation has its own power. We are part of the creation, and God speaks to us in the way that we can cope with, in accord with our nature as created beings. It is not strange that God should speak in this way. He is, after all, the creator and he speaks creation. God's way of speaking is creative. In fact, he himself became part of the creation, in the flesh of Jesus.

The power of the sun is the power of God. There is a Hebridean custom for men to doff their caps to the sun in the morning and for women to bend the knee to the moon at night. It is the sort of custom which seems to be open to the charge of pantheism, but rather it is a direct recognition of God's presence in creation. There was never any confusion, as their prayers show, between the creator God and his creation.

Healing

I came across a wonderful meditation by George Tyrrell (a twentieth-century Jesuit). It is the incident, in Luke 5, where a woman was cured of a haemorrhage from which she had suffered for many years. She stood at the edge of the crowd surrounding Jesus, unwilling to make a public proclamation of her condition and said to herself: 'If only I can touch the hem of his garment I will be healed.' As she did so Christ felt the power go out from him. Tyrrell makes a correspondence between the garments of Christ and nature:

So everywhere Scripture represents Nature as the garment of God, as the guise in which he has chosen to walk and talk with us upon the earth. It is God who shines in the

sun, moon, and stars, who rages in the storm, who con-
sumes in the fire, who thunders from the clouds, who
clothes Himself in glorious apparel, girds Himself with
strength, robes Himself in light, veils Himself in the
clouds . . . Nature, then, is the garment of God; and . . .
we can draw near from behind, and touch with trembling
hope the fringe of His vesture, and be healed of our
infirmities.

(from a meditation in *Nova et Vetera*)

It is not unusual for a person who is stressed in mind and
body to find solace and even healing in the arms of nature.
Once, when feeling resentful and angry at being (as I
thought) 'banished' to Shetland, I found comfort and
strength by walking on the moors and by the sea cliffs there.

The Irish journalist Brian Keenan, who had been kept as
a hostage in Lebanon, and being severely injured in body and
soul by the experience, relates how he found his peace of
mind by wandering in the wild country of the west of Ireland.

Labour in creation

God laboured in creation, and continues to do so. It would
be a mistake to see nature in terms of the soft arms of a
mother cradling a child. The volcano that swept down on the
people of Goma did not bring comfort, nor the earthquakes
that regularly shatter towns and cities. The brokenness of
nature and the fact that nevertheless it is the work of love are
dealt with in another chapter.

The Centre cannot hold: the cord
that binds us to creation
seems to be bitten through;

and we, like satellites cut loose
from the Controller's desk, wander
in endless waste, creating waste. Yet
there comes One who spreads wide
his aching arms and draws all things
unto himself, back to the centre, back
to the path of love.

To stop and listen in silence,
to stop and look in silence,
to stop and feel in silence
is the beginning of wisdom.

To hear a petal slowly unfolding
body and mind, both
must be in abyssal silence;
to sense the growing of a tree,
time itself must stand motionless.
Only in silence
can true prayer be born,
there where past and future meet.
For what has gone and what will come
are clamorous, demanding and anxious.
Silence is only present.
It is still, it is now.
It can never be anything but itself.
It makes no demands,
except that absolute demand –
to let go, release the self.
God is the pause between two thoughts,
the inner being of matter
where silence reigns,
the mystery at the heart of creation.

❀❀❀

3
The Labour of Love
A spirituality of brokenness

Ecce homo: Behold the man

Pilate brought him out in front of the crowd. He had been lashed in a way that could kill a man, then mocked and a crown of thorns rammed down on his skull. A purple mocking-cloak was thrown over his bleeding body, and it was in this state that Pilate called out from the balcony, 'Look, I am going to bring him out to you . . .'. When Jesus appeared, Pilate gestured towards him and said, 'Here is the man!'

The man! Stay with that image. Christ, draped in the cloak, a rod of mock authority stuck into this hand, the crown bleeding down his face. And Pilate saying, Here is the man. I have always been struck by that statement. It says far more than it seems to. This is not just *a* man, not just any man, but *the* man. Christ standing there represents the whole of humankind. He is the man. And what he represents is a race that suffers, from injustice, aggression and brutality. The human race is a broken article.

Isaiah had said of the Suffering Servant of Yahweh:

the crowds were appalled on seeing him, such a disfigured figure, scarcely human . . . Without beauty, without majesty we saw him, his looks no longer appealing; despised, rejected by people, a man of sorrows and familiar with suffering, a man to make people screen their faces; he was despised and we took no account of him.

(Isaiah 52.14; 53.3)

In this chapter we will try to be aware that

1 Suffering is a part of the human lot. To refuse to face or accept it is to refuse the price of salvation; it can be what saves us.
2 The awareness of suffering suggests that we have to change what we think of as 'being human' and our image of God.
3 God's death on a cross puts him *inside* rather than *outside* the experience of suffering in our lives.

Nature red in tooth and claw

It is possible to be lulled into cooing the praises of nature without facing its dark side. No consideration of creation and the mysteries locked into it are complete or plausible without recognition of its negative factors. We can swoon at the song of the blackbird and the aeronautics of jackdaws, overlooking meantime the misery of starvation and thirst, the genocide that has dogged our human history, and the apparently endless pain and suffering borne by our race. Much of the cause lies at the feet of human sin, but not all. There are catastrophes and disasters which are not precipitated by our greed and rapaciousness – which does not in any way justify the catastrophes and disasters which *are* brought on by our sinfulness.

Deliver us from suffering

A great deal of human effort is expended in trying to avoid

— 39 —

pain and discomfort. We want a world free of suffering. Medical research is dedicated to the elimination of disease and, with it, pain. Pneumonia and TB used to carry off thousands yearly; now they can be treated with relative ease. Yet we do not seem ever to attain the goal of a pain-free life.

We seem to want a toil-free world as well. Unending leisure is the goal. Our dwellings are more and more crowded with washing machines, vacuum cleaners, microwave cookers and many other devices for 'having it now if not before'. We have invented methods of travel to reduce the 'travail' of travel, making it swift and comfortable. So successful have we been that the roads are choked, the airways are beginning to choke and the beaches in the sunny parts of the world are full of people almost tripping over each other.

We consider that a perfect world would have no suffering, no toil. A picture, in fact, of the garden of Eden before the fall?

Somehow, it doesn't happen. Diseases are eradicated, but new ones appear, or the old ones in more virulent form. We still die, and alone. Our lives are just as rushed as they ever were, perhaps more. Ease of life cannot be equated with happiness. It has been argued that a created universe, being subject (as all matter is) to change, cannot be perfect. Hence, it will always be subject to pain and suffering. Our experience of love involves suffering and patience.

Behold the man

Yet we are right to try to eradicate pain. It is, of itself, an evil. The distortions of the human frame caused by disease and famine are surely not what was intended by the creator?

We encounter one of the paradoxes of the gospel here. Christ cured lepers, helped the blind to see, loosed the tongues of the dumb, and straightened those who were crippled. He freed those who were held in the bonds of mental torture. For a short time (less than three years) and in a small place he healed the sick. He probably healed fewer people than a large city hospital would cure in a month nowadays. Yet it was obvious that that was what he saw as part of his work on earth. He was giving a sign, of what the Father would wish to see in creation, an opening of the gates of the Kingdom.

But he himself suffered. So much so, that his suffering is equated with his redemptive power. He is, in Celtic terms, 'Son of the wounds'.

A broken world

Suffering is a great disarmer. It tears down our barriers, removes piece by piece the suit of armour that keeps us safe from the slings and arrows of outrageous fortune. It dislodges from our grasp the sword in our hand that gives us the power to be self-sufficient, and tears from our hands the reins which guide our own destinies. Consequently, it throws us, defenceless, into the hands of God. And yet, for many, it is precisely the time when God is angrily discounted. 'How can he do this to me? I trusted him and now look what I get!' It is easy to blame God. I came across, in some notes I had made, lines which were doing just that. I had been walking in the park, brooding on television news pictures of scenes from the war in Croatia.

> Hacked to mere stumps
> the bush-stem cowers by the path
> like a guillotined criminal.
> Can these bones live and grow again?
> Have faith! The Gardener knows his trade
> and the fruit of his pruning.

In a subterranean ward,
below the bombed-out streets,
the news-shot scans a bed.
Relentlessly, the lens moves down
the woman's tender body and lights,
without pause or mercy,
on the bandaged stumps that were her legs,
severed unceremoniously
by a Serbian shell. Have faith!
The Ruthless Gardener in the sky
is doing his grim pruning!

Dire words! I think now I would want to add:

Look now upon the figure on the cross
and tell me what you see?
Is this the Ruthless Gardener in the sky,
or some God-orphaned body
cut down in its prime? And why?
It is we who are the pruners, not he.

The wounds of the world may well be the entry points of God's love for us.

Not the body beautiful

Brokenness is not a rare factor in human experience. Far from it. It is so usual, in one form or another, that Jean Vanier, who started the L'Arche communities to care for those who are disabled, reckons that our usual image of what 'human' means cannot be the healthy, fit, beautiful body that we think it to be. If we think in these terms then to be human means to be healthy. Illness then becomes the enemy, to be suppressed and avoided. Sick people are pushed out of sight. For health to become the be all and end all of life in this way is to rob the human being of the true strength of his humanity. Health is not the meaning of human life.

Paradoxically, the stress on health leads to a great fear of illness.

A new perspective

We have to change perspective, and cease to judge our worthwhileness by performance and physical beauty. That is how the advertisements would have us think and estimate, but a truer picture is of a world of ordinary beings, many in wheelchairs, the aged, the sick, broken in mind or body. Such a plethora of programmes on the television are about sickness and hospitals!

Our TV screen gives us at one and the same time a picture of a world of people hungry and desolate, often fleeing from war and destruction, alongside advertisements for helps to achieve the body beautiful and the life plentiful. Pain and suffering are so much part of our world that one writer reckoned we must alter our estimation of what is human, our idea of what sort of God we must reckon on, and how he interacts with us, if we are to accommodate these terrible experiences into our world-picture.

Suffering can attack us from outside ourselves, or from within. It can be of body, or of mind or spirit. Ill-fortune can land on our doorstep suddenly and without warning. For some in the North of Ireland it came in the form of a bomb blast, or bullets from a gun. For others, as a bill they could not pay; or announcing a bereavement. There are myriad ways in which misfortune can turn a corner and confront us.

The misfortunes that strike from within are perhaps often more severe: natural failings, physical defects, intellectual and moral weakness, which can limit the living of our lives, and infect our joy. The diminishments of old age spare no-one, and end inevitably in death.

To be human is to suffer.

Choice sufferings

People suffer for what they believe in, what they stand for. That is why Christ suffered. That is what martyrs suffer for. They suffer for the choices they make, not that they choose suffering, but because what they choose involves having to suffer for that choice. They suffer for freedom, they suffer because they love. It is a necessary consequence, in this life, of our devotion, our promises, of who we are. We remember those who stood up for human rights and suffered prison and death for their convictions.

In our time, with medical advances, we are intolerant of suffering, feeling it is our 'right' not to suffer. But others say, it is our right to suffer! Insistence that we have a 'right' not to suffer can lead to euthanasia.

Pain, brokenness, failure, is a mode of intense love such as Christ's own suffering was.

God the provider?

Do I expect God to be the provider of the healthy and plentiful life? Do I, in Old Testament terms, equate wealth with blessing? Perhaps wealth is a blessing, but God does not always fit this picture. Even in the Old Testament a new realization was beginning to shape: God is on the side of the poor and the broken and the needy. 'My ways are not your ways . . .' God is 'good' when we see the splendour of Mount Tabor; 'not-so-good' when the following of him leads to hardship and suffering. The Bible is a story of a broken and despised people calling on a God who is made most accessible in pathos and tears. There are moments of triumph in this picture of God, but the dominant note is vulnerability. A vulnerable God! Have we any time for that?

Brokenness, of course, is not an end in itself: it is love on the way to completion. This God is good news only to those who are broken. You have to be emptied to be filled.

Grace as a harsh truth

That truth, that God can fill us with his life only if we are emptied of the opposite, forces us to reassess how grace works, that is, how God reacts with us in our lives. Do we have the conviction that grace is the life of God flowing into us like petrol into a car, to make us feel good, and strong, and easing our path in life? If we do, I think we can be in for a shock! Grace is more like the crack that knocked Saul off his horse on the road to Damascus. It can be a harsh reality, something to shock us out of our complacency and remove our security. This is often so unacceptable that we cannot equate it with the work of a good God.

Rahner talks of the two-edged sword of faith that brings fragmentation in us rather than ease. Grace is our attempt to serve God even when it means dying and negation. It is the action of grace when I do something for another without any thanks or recognition of what I do. Yet our nature, derived from God, must have a capacity and congeniality for this grace.

Passivities

What Teilhard calls the 'passivities' of our existence, the things we have to undergo rather than do ourselves, form half of our lives. We prefer the activities because we like to be doing. But these 'passivities' are immeasurably wider and deeper. We are beset by bits of ill-fortune – we can look back on our lives and see them, like blotches on a face – the sudden accidents that immobilize us (especially when they result in the junking of our car!), the bits of bad luck that destroy our peace of mind (mortgage trouble?), the microbes that steal away our health, the bereavements that take away loved ones, and many other such things. We can, perhaps, survive the removal of possessions, because we can always imagine getting them back or buying replacements. But there are worse things, the natural failings we are subject to, physical disabilities which make our lives more difficult to bear. Dudley Moore had great talent, both as comedian and musician, but struggled to overcome the effects of the club foot he was born with, and his lack of height.

Can we hope to find God in all this diminishment? Such things seem to contradict his very creativity. Yet, if we refuse to look for him there we are blocking off a direct channel to him. Whatever we may suffer we know that Christ has been there before us. The things we undergo are signposts on the way.

God's shock: the cross

The crucifix is one shock to our complacency. It has always been a central emblem of Christianity and yet was referred to by St Paul as a 'stumbling block' for many people in his time. An 'almighty' God could not be subjected to this!

I suspect that it may still be a shock to many today. Either it is simply an outward sign that bears little meaning; or, if taken seriously, is simply adding to the weight of human misery. Does it seem to glorify suffering for its own sake? That is not what it is all about. We don't have to impose suffering on the human condition, it is there already.

God shares our brokenness

The crucifixion is the recognition that God in Christ did not hesitate to come and share our brokenness.

> Though he was of the divinity he didn't cling to his equality with God but emptied himself (of glory) and took on the condition of a slave, to become as we all are; even to the extent of accepting death, the death of a cross.
>
> (Philippians 2.6–9)

This is not just an affair of the Son of God. A mother suffers in her son. So God too suffers in his Son. In becoming one of us Jesus entered into all the labyrinthine complications of our humanity, sinfulness and all (though not himself sinful). The cross is the expression of evil, of human depravity. The twisting of the good. Even so, Christ saw his suffering as glorious. 'Now is the hour of my glorification' (John).

From the inside

What characterizes the attitude of both Ignatius and the Celts is the total commitment to Christ. It is stated in Ignatius and may or may not be in the Celts, but their actions are unmistakable.

> The experience of the Passion is from the inside – not looking on from the outside, not just 'I'm glad you did this' but rather 'I want it to happen to me too. I want to suffer with you and so rise with you.' This is a mark of love. If someone you deeply love is suffering you want somehow to share it. This cannot be arrived at by work; it is the grace of God.
>
> (from unpublished notes on the *Spiritual Exercises* by Ron Darwen, SJ)

Ignatius at the cross

Try praying before the cross by imagining yourself really there, standing with Mary and John beneath that horrid gibbet. Don't try to 'do' anything, just be there, participating by presence in the death of Christ. This participation prepares us for the event in our own lives. It may involve the experience of darkness, misunderstanding, dryness in prayer . . .

Whatever a person suffers, Jesus has touched and sanctified that abyss. He may not have shared exactly the same sufferings as we do (he did not grow old, lose a child, sin) but has searched every pain in intensity. The suffering of the Son of God, mocked, deserted and godforsaken, offers a home for everyone's sorrow. You do not walk alone.

The passion is still happening

Although the contemplation of the cross is a one-to-one encounter of the person with Christ, nevertheless the whole world must come into it. Jesus's passion was salvific; and so my joining with him is also part of salvation of the race. Perhaps the most characteristic grace of the passion is, appropriately, compassion, a 'suffering with' another person. This spiritual empathy becomes itself a 'passion' for the one who is praying, involving him or her in Christ's passion. It must be an expression of intense love, not a form of masochism. Given that this is so, it will transform the way we see the passion. It becomes a contemplative union. In this way, through the prayer and action of those who follow his footsteps, Christ works in our world today, suffering now as he did then, and in us, for the redemption of the world. This is the perception of the Christian Celts and of Ignatius.

Crucifixion

Our search for security may mean trust in doctrines and

dogmas, and the devotion of statues and symbols. The crucifixion shattered that trust. The very God on whom we place security and dependence forsook Jesus on the cross. The crucifixion spelled the end of all human ambition, hope and trust in what is normally termed 'God': the supreme good, supreme righteousness, the bastion of protection. Such things are done to death on the cross. Anything which promises permanence and stability in this life is hung on the cross. This is what distinguishes Christianity from other religions. The old way of thinking must be forsaken, as Jesus was on the cross, and a new way established. Christ was the victim of religion, of society and the state, the victim of sin; and by dying he became the brother of all such victims.

Emptied to be filled

Christ was 'emptied' on the cross. He was emptied physically, his senses pulverized, his clothes torn off, the blood drained from his body. This was prepared for by his manner of life, lived in total simplicity which he described when he said: 'Foxes have holes and the birds of the air their nests but the son of man has nowhere to lay his head.' Deprived of home, reputation and, finally, most terrifying, the support of his Father: 'My God , my God, why have you abandoned me?'

Suffering turns us in on ourselves. One aching tooth holds our attention riveted onto that spot, to the exclusion of all larger concerns of our lives. I had gout in my big toe recently, and for a time my whole life was circumscribed by that big toe. Pain drags our whole attention towards it. Yet, on the cross Christ, going through the most painful death, was able to look at his tormentors and say, 'Father, forgive them, they do not know what they are doing!' It takes an immense effort of turning away from self and self-concerns to do that. Christ, in his suffering, was fulfilling the nature of the Trinity which is one of going out from self to the other. Each person gives totally to the others. In fact, J. V. Taylor has used the term 'In-Othering' to describe it. Theologians have used the Greek word *kenosis* for it, meaning a going out from oneself, an emptying. That is what love is all about, giving to another, giving self away. Not that the Trinity is one great suffering machine, but in our human lives we may have to be forced out of ourselves, such is our tendency to self-concentration and self-love.

Suffering dissolves our dreams and hopes, deconstructs our plans and breaks the walls of security. It is an emptying, and as such is a living out of that *kenosis* of the Trinity.

Letting go

In some sense, in some way, it is the emptying that we too have to undergo. We talk, in this, of 'dying to the world'. We need to be careful of our use of terms here. Is it not true that we come to God in and through our createdness, in and through the incarnation, in and through our bodies and the creation around us? How then can we be asked not to love these things?

Maybe it is more a question of the sort of love. The only full love of the world is the love that the creator has for it, and only by allowing ourselves to enter into that love can we be fully children of the earth. In order to do that we have to strip ourselves of the superficial love of created things which tends to be selfish and grasping. We do this with Christ on the cross. Emptied, we can receive that love of God which embraces the world and all created things. There is a necessary emptying of the person in order to receive God. It is like clearing a room of junk to receive a new occupant, a special visitor.

'Letting go' of things we love, people we love, letting go of a situation, or a place, are inevitable elements of our life. We are continually 'emptied' of our inner furniture, and this is the space that God will fill, if allowed. We may resent the wrench, and try to avoid it, but life shows this to be impossible.

In the prayer 'Anima Christi', Ignatius asks: 'On each of my dyings shed your light and your love.' Perhaps it is that these little dyings, which recur throughout our lives, are the way in which we are prepared, by an exercise of abandonment, for a love which Christ first showed us.

The Celtic sense of the cross

For the Celtic Church the Christ that they sensed to be with them was also the whole Christ. Theirs was not a Christianity of ease. They were as much with his crucifixion as with his life and resurrection. Life, after all, is a patchwork of birth, maturity, joy and sadness, death and resurrection. Any part of life has these elements and results in a certain attitude of acceptance of whatever comes, whether it be joy or pain. 'A fine day, thank God', is accepted as readily as 'A fine, soft day', when it is raining. When placed in the same frame as the crucifixion of Jesus, even pain and suffering can be accepted as part of God's saving of the world.

Celtic gloom?

The crucifixion seemed to be compatible with their history and even with their mythology, which contains many tales of suffering and sadness, such as Deirdre of the Sorrows. Celtic descriptions of the passion of Christ have a warmth and personal touch which gives the impression that it was something accepted into the lives of ordinary people. The modern song 'The Thorn Tree' is an example of this. While the thorn tree was feared by many, Katy Ryan had a dream in which Christ complained that this should be so, since the crown he wore was woven from branches of the thorn tree.

The Celtic atmosphere of the crucified is a *personal* thing, as though they had themselves stood there at the foot of the cross, as intimate as in a dream.

There is a legend of a king of Ulster, Conchobor (or Conor) Mac Nessa who had a ball of shot lodged in his brain after a battle. He was warned to avoid sudden movement or even emotion, which could dislodge the ball and kill him. But one day the sky was stormy and gloomy and he asked the wise men the reason, and they told him the news of the crucifixion of the Son of God. The king jumped up in a rage at this terrible happening and began to hack at a tree, with the inevitable result. Dislodging the ball, he fell dead, as it were at the foot of the cross. Christ's death was a personal tragedy.

The Celtic attitude to the body of Christ was shown in references to the cross. The sacred body, the body that was crucified, is made welcome.

A sense of the sacredness of the body is enhanced in it.

Blathmac's poem

There is a poem from the mid-eighth century by a man called Blathmac, in which he expresses the sense of affront at what was done to Christ,

> shocked at the way he was seized and beaten, struck with stick and fist;
> shocked at the fact that it was his own 'mother-kin' that killed him, that spat on him, the creator;
> shocked at his carrying of his cross, and crucifixion between criminals;

shocked at a crown of thorns on the beautiful head (there
is nothing beautiful to please our eyes, says Isaiah 53);
shocked at the nails through hands and feet;
shocked at the mocking of the king, the stripping, the casting lots;
shocked at the piercing with the lance of Longinus.

Not just a sense of outrage, but the ravaging of the beauty
of God, the beautiful body that they stripped. The body
given up, and the blood spilled, is always for St John symbol of the Eucharist. And always the mixture of pain and
tenderness:

> At the dawn chorus did they begin Thy crucifixion,
> O swanlike cheek!
>
> (from Esther de Waal,
> *A World Made Whole*)

The suffering of the mother was part of that of the son, each
suffering for the other.

King of the Friday

Blathmac's poetry is couched in terms of horror at the crucifixion, but also of love. He described how nature itself
entered into the crucifixion when the sun hid its light in
mourning, darkness covered the heavens and the sea cried
out in anguish. The rocks burst open and the whole land
was in gloom because they were God's creatures and were
keening for their creator. This sense, that the actions of
Christ and his death influence the whole of creation, is
typical of their unified sense of God and creation and
became integrated into their everyday lives. Christ became
'King of the Friday', and thereafter Friday became accepted

as the best day to sow seed in the field, anticipating the resurrection of Christ and the germination of the seed.

Nature was involved in the death of Christ. The Celts were aware of the writing of St Paul in Colossians, that Christ is a cosmic figure, the linchpin of creation. They knew that Christ's suffering and death were the means by which our race was saved; and they came to understand, with the Christian world, that their own suffering was incorporated into that of Christ. The cross became an integral part of their lives, and to find that their suffering was not just a meaningless horror, but had been entered into by God himself and was thereby incorporated into salvation history, was something that gave them meaning and joy.

As Ignatius asks us to contemplate a God who is working in creation, so the Celt accepts that creation will entail its degree of pain and labour.

Three martyrdoms

We are used to the idea of martyrs for causes, suffering in the interests of justice. Christians have always seen martyrdom as perseverance in clinging to their beliefs, even if it meant death.

The Celtic acceptance of suffering is shown in the fact that they thought in terms of *three* sorts of martyrdom! They expanded the ideal of martyrdom to include any form of giving oneself for Christ and their faith. One reason for this is that the Celts were not, on the whole, subjected to martyrdom in the sense that other Christians were. The Irish Celts were not persecuted for their faith by the Roman emperors and so were deprived of the benefit of the blood of martyrdom which formed such an important element of the early Christian ideal. They had to 'invent' it!

While retaining the 'red' martyrdom of dying for the faith

(and one or two did end in this way – Donnan on the island of Eigg was decapitated by a Pictish queen!) they considered that forsaking land and home was a form of 'white' martyrdom, as they called it. The third kind was what they called 'green', the martyrdom of living a life of asceticism for Christ in the state of life in which one found oneself. Each of these represented a way of entering into the 'stripping' that Christ suffered on the cross and became for them a martyrdom of the heart.

⚜⚜⚜

If I have offered you the breath that gives me life,
if I have followed faithful to your call,
if you became my love, my hope, my voice,
if I have trodden, step by step with you,
then will your footprints lead me to your cross.
There is no life but with its root in death.
We come of an afflicted race of pain
and suffering begets us all our days.
The pain of failure is redeeming grace.
Success is not.

When the side of Christ was pierced by the lance
it seemed the whole creation suffered pain
and was scarred. Nature became
red in tooth and claw, marked by the lance
of our sin and shame. Blood flowed
like the red hot lava streams
that poured onto the homes of Goma.
People die, a blood-lust spirit lives
and roams around the earth, seeking
whom it may devour.

Yet the same wound
let flow a stream of blood that washed
our world of sin, and opened up
a tributary vein that led from us to God,
an artery that fed from God to us.
We gash creation with our spiky sins,
yet God has turned it to a happy fault.

4
Enfleshing the Mystery
A spirituality of the here and now

In the bustle of the streets of Calcutta no-one would have noticed the dying man but for one thing – he was being held and cradled by a young woman dressed in the sari that distinguished one of Mother Theresa's nuns. She tried to make him as comfortable as possible for his last hours on earth, and when he died she made arrangements for him to be taken away. Then, sadly, she returned to the convent. It was not unusual work for her to be doing, but she invested it with a deep spiritual meaning. She explained to one of her companions, 'I have been holding the body of Christ for the past two hours!'

In such simple terms she expressed the profound mystery of the incarnation and resurrection of Christ.

God moved to 'enflesh' the mystery of his being by taking flesh and being born of Mary. We too need, in various ways, to bring the reality of God to life for ourselves. In this chapter I want to think about 'enfleshing', that is, providing ways in to the different aspects of mystery in our lives and in our faith. In doing so we will encounter these points:

1 Human life needs mystery.
2 There is mystery all around us, not least in our own bodies.

3 Christian life centres on the mystery of the incarnation of Christ.

4 We need to clothe the mystery of our own lives, and the mystery of Christ's life by our imagination.

Mystery and wonder

Wonder is the ante-room to the sense of mystery. Without mystery our world becomes dull and listless, a bundle of dry facts, stuff waiting to be woven into cushions for our comfort. But the comfort itself is dull and listless.

Mystery excites the soul, stimulates the mind. It is a sense of something deep at the heart of being which we cannot as yet fully understand, and so it draws us deeper. It will do this only if we recognize the limitations of our knowledge or the very impossibility of our knowing. Being led deeper is of the essence of the life of the soul. 'Science', said a friend of mine, 'is heartless.' Fortunately, at least in my experience, scientists themselves are mostly not heartless.

Ultimately, the sense of mystery stems from our origin in the Trinity, the supreme mystery. The world's meaning and 'direction' is like the ball thrown by a juggler into the air which returns to his hand infallibly by the very way it is thrown, by the power and direction it is given by the hand of the juggler. The juggler is the creating God.

Mystery of the body

To experience mystery in our lives we need look no further than our own bodies. Scientists have done great things in discovering more and more of its wonders. This can lead to an attitude which thinks of the body as though it were just a machine, which can be explained fully by research. But the deeper we search, the more the mystery. We are made in the image of God, and embody part of the mystery of the Trinity, and since body and soul go together there will be layer on layer of deeper mystery to plumb. Only the Divine Plumber knows it all!

We need to wonder as we contemplate the body and its development.

Body matters

The body has been formed in a process reproduced millions of times in the world when the fertilized cell embeds in the womb and begins to divide madly in geometric progression (called mitosis) 1, 2, 4, 8, 16, 32, etc., until a little ball of cells is formed which hollows out.

You would think, to look at it, that it was just an undifferentiated blob of cellular matter. But these cells are not undifferentiated. Already distinctions are being made, choices established. For the miracle is that each of these little cells knows exactly what it has to do, and where it has to go. The cells in one area will form a nerve tube, others go to form muscles. They know where they should be! With purpose they move towards their rightful place. How do they know where to go? The information is carried within each cell.

The movements become complex. A set of developments called 'gastrulation' now sculptures the hollow ball of cells into a complex 3-dimensional organism with inner, outer and middle layers of tissue. There is no architect present to say, 'You go there', 'You come over here'! These cells are predestined. They move with an ordered irrevocability. Each of the layers will give rise to particular parts of the body, the outside (ectoderm) developing skin, hair, glands, the nervous system and sense organs. The middle layer (mesoderm) forms connective tissue, muscle, and the inner layer (endoderm) forms the lining of the gut, of the liver, thyroid, etc. But even as the three germ layers arise, their cells are already committed to these distinctions. Should they be wrongly placed, a deformed body results.

At the moment of birth, systems that had been in operation during the formation of the embryo are instantly shut down and a new set of systems for life in the air are switched on. So the miracle continues.

This is what took place in the embryo of Jesus Christ Our Lord.

The body has a central role in salvation. No body, no salvation. Through the body we contact God. St John's First Epistle speaks of 'the One we have heard, and we have seen with our own eyes; that we have watched and touched with our hands: the Word, who is life'.

Body speaks of a complex of relationships. That complex is mirroring the complexity of the world, and human interrelationships. Sin spells disruption of these connections, on a global and on an individual level, dividing peoples, nations, human beings from others, and ourselves within ourselves. Body becomes divided from spirit and mind dominates the whole.

Bio-spiritual focusing

The body is central to *bio-spiritual focusing*, a system of awareness of what is happening in our bodies as reflecting the issues in our lives that are affecting us. Body is the temple of spirit, it is home, our familiar place. Yet the disconnection we can see in the world, the disconnection of people among themselves, nation from nation, the separation between the body and the earth – all these 'disconnections' have roots in the body itself.

The other day I found myself writing down a sense of spring which I felt in the weather (alas, after that the weather reverted to winter!).

> Winter
> still clutched the soil.
> Cold winds had not abated
> and ribs of snow still traced
> the contours of the hills.
> On a high tree,
> scarcely visible to the eye,
> a blackbird raised his voice,
> pouring out an anthem
> of triumphant praise
> against the cold, grey sky.
> Then I knew,
> with an avalanche of feeling,
> that it was spring. No flowers,
> no breaking buds or leaves
> proclaimed this truth. Yet this thin
> and distant voice released in me
> a flood of atmosphere, a world
> of memory, and joy and hope.
> Such a tiny spark
> to light a conflagration!

That is a way we explain focusing. Some stimulus, a word, a smell, enters our sense perception. The tip of the iceberg is where that little distant sound plugs in, descending almost by seepage into the basement below, spreading out into that great chamber of delight, the memories, the love, the excitement, the desires, the pain, the expectation of companionship and wonder. It even brought in its train a song,

'Down in the glen' which spread out in its turn and even now gives me a feeling of longing as I write this.

It descends, without reference to our head–brain, into a whole world of stored-up experience in our bodies, and sets off a reaction, re-igniting feelings there that may have been long forgotten. I was walking once on the Isle of Lewis with a friend of mine and I stopped suddenly, sniffing the air.

'What is that smell?' My friend looked at me and said, 'It is the smell of turf burning.' And so it was. It brought back in me part of my childhood spent in Ireland. The scent of the burning turf conjured up a whole world and all the wonders of that time.

As often as not, though, the strongest reactions are negative ones. A quarrel with someone has left me rough and spiky, like a hedgehog, and that works its way down into my body, perhaps feeding into a story of animosity, which in turn may have undertones of interiority.

Bio-spiritual focusing is derived from the work of Eugene Gendlin, PhD, who studied psychotherapy under Carl Rogers in America. He works on the assumption that the body has a form of knowing which is different from that of the brain. This knowledge which the body contains can be contacted by paying attention to the feelings within, and accepting them and granting them permission to be there, and welcoming them, even if they are negative to our sensibility. When, for instance, we are seething with anger there will be direct feelings within our bodies. If these are given care and acceptance the body will gradually work with them and modify them in its own way, enabling us to live better with them. The body *knows*. Not the logical thinking of the brain, but a knowing nevertheless. An older, kinder knowledge.

Spend time, perhaps in the morning when you wake up, simply becoming aware of what you are feeling, what is going on in your body, and as you locate the feeling accept it and welcome it, and do not fight it even if it is negative. Just stay with that awareness.

We have treated the body like a yokel that is dumb. In fact it is a fountain of knowledge, a well of wisdom and a history of experience waiting to help us. Like the books on the shelf it waits for us to look inside.

Bio-spiritual focusing helps practitioners to do that. It could well be that this is at the root of Ignatian discernment. Ignatius found that his body reaction to a particular thought or action was an indicator of how to act rightly.

Incarnation

This chapter is called 'Enfleshing the Mystery'. The way God 'enfleshed' his mystery was precisely by 'taking flesh', by becoming a human being. That is what the word 'incarnation' means. Being composed of body and soul we need something, some*body*, that we can see and touch.

A friend related how he had been visiting relatives and having an evening dinner with them. The little daughter of the house had been put to bed, but appeared in her nightie during the dinner. The solicitous mother told her they had said their prayers to God the Father and Son and Holy Spirit, and so she could go to sleep now. But the little girl replied, 'But Mummy, I need something with skin on it!' That's exactly it. She might have been quoting from St John's first letter quoted above: 'Something . . . that we have heard, and we have seen with our own eyes; that we have watched and touched with our hands: the Word, who is life'.

Jesus showed concern for bodies all his public life. He knew the crucial importance of the body for the salvation of the person. His touch cured leprosy, epilepsy, paralysis. The bodily touch made people *whole*.

The woman who was bent double
(based on Luke 13.10–17)

Jesus was teaching, on a sabbath day, in a synagogue. A woman was there who had been crippled for the past eighteen years; she was bent double and quite unable to stand up straight. When Jesus saw her he called her over and said, 'Woman, you are freed from your sickness.' He placed his hands on her and at once she straightened up, and glorified God.

The synagogue official, however, was angry because Jesus had healed someone on the sabbath day, and he said to the people present, 'You can work on six days of the week. Come for healing on one of those days, not on the sabbath.' Jesus turned on him and said, 'How hypocritical you lot are! Wouldn't you untether your cow or your donkey on the sabbath and take it out for watering? And here is this woman, a daughter of Abraham who has been held bound by Satan these eighteen years past – wasn't it right to untie her bonds on the sabbath day?' When he said this, his enemies hung their heads in shame, while all the people were overjoyed at all the wonders he worked.

The body was bent double, confining the woman's sight of creation to a circle at her feet. In straightening her spine Jesus gave her back pride in her own self, a glimpse of the wonders of creation all around her, and her dignity. She could look the world in the eye again. Body and spirit were healed.

Matter matters

Spirit is matter seen from within, matter is spirit seen from without.

Christianity must hold a special place for the body, that temple of the spirit. Like Samuel we live in this temple. If ever there were a doubt in Christianity of the central place of the body, then the incarnation answers it, that all but incredible mystery of God's dedication to creation to the extent that he became part of it. Here was a creator who loved what he had made, as parents will love what they have brought into being. We cannot elect to be born, or not to be, our fate is decided for us for better or worse. But God *could* choose. Of all the myriad possibilities open to him he chose to become one of us. Did he come 'trailing clouds of glory'? An alien stepping out of a flying saucer? No. He was announced to shepherds in a field of sheep droppings, telling them to go to a stable smelling of cows and straw to find an infant born to poor parents and wrapped, for want of anything better, in swaddling clothes. Not very propitious. Something very ordinary. We often speak in terms of God 'condescending' to our condition; but is it not rather a case of God's wonder at the miracle of his own son and the loving cooperation of Mary?

Body expresses soul?

The soul is the form of the body. The two go together. We used to refer to the body as the Temple of the Holy Spirit. It is the temple of our own spirit too, and the place where our soul meets the world and reacts with it. It is where we interact with the earth and other people, where we act upon the outside, and the outside comes in upon us. So, in a real sense it is a sacred place. That is why St Paul wishes that we treat it as sacred, and not abuse it. Respect for the body of others is contained in that.

Transfiguration

Jesus, in a special way, bridges the gap between the two worlds. In his risen body we see this clearly. But there were also certain times in his ministerial life when the divinity shone through the humanity. When he was baptized a voice came from above, 'This is my Son, the Beloved. Listen to him.' But the clearest example is the transfiguration, when for a time the imaginal world was visible and the thin veil became transparent. In a mysterious way the body of Christ became translucent, and the Spirit glowed through like the sun through thin cloud. For a time the interpenetration of spirit and matter was the very sign of the enfleshment of the mystery of Christ. Though they did not know it then, it was for the three apostles present, a preview of the resurrected body of the Lord.

Celtic wholeness

Our religion has become too cognitive. The Celts were never in danger of that. They imagined, they sensed, they intimated their faith.

The body is a nurse. Becoming aware of the feelings present is a channel into body knowledge, tapping into a store, a mine of experience. To embrace that feeling with care, assuring the body that we will hold the baby, cuddle it, rock it, is to open the door of the well of knowledge stored in the body. Not that the hurts are necessarily removed. The body is not so much a healer as a carer, a nurse. It is in fact a bearer. Christ was the one who carried our woes, our sins, our wounds. So the body is for us a carrier that knows how to shoulder the wounded self.

Risen body

The risen Lord comes in as 'consoler', says Ignatius. All experience can be cashed in him. This book is brought together in him.

Much of the Gospel account deals with the disappearance of the Lord's body. When he appears to the disciples he points to his body. This highlights the special place of the body in spirituality. The incarnation shows this, even by the word itself. It is a down-to-earth spirituality. The description above of the movement of cells in the formation of a body underlines the human reality of Christ, for that is how he must have been formed in the womb of Mary. The flesh, as theologians used to say, is the hinge of salvation.

In the Risen Lord we confirm our basic attitude to creation and belief in a 'good' God. We are engaged in a spirituality of creation, on this earth.

The upper room

Try being present in the upper room with the apostles and Mary after the crucifixion. Settle yourself for prayer in a suitable place, be still for a few minutes, and then read the text of John 20, verses 19 to 29. Put the book aside, and enter into the scene in your imagination. You are locked into the room for fear of being recognized as followers of the crucified criminal. Get a sense of the fear, the tension. Some are sitting, others prowl around like hunted deer, restless and not knowing where to hide, and totally preoccupied with sadness, fear and the failure of hope. What are you doing, saying, thinking, feeling?

Suddenly Jesus himself is present, standing among you.

What is your reaction? Suddenly there is an electric awareness and a switch of attention. What is this spectre? Are you
seeing things? Even Jesus' reassurances don't fully work.
'Touch me', he says. 'Satisfy yourselves that I'm no ghost.
What are you so afraid of? Look, my hands, my feet. It is I.
Touch me and you'll see. A ghost isn't made of flesh and
bones like this!'

Using the senses is an invitation to prove to ourselves that
this risen body is real, is flesh and blood. Jesus adds the further proof by asking for food and eating it – a very bodily
activity! Thomas, coming in late and missing the occasion,
refuses to believe and had to be convinced, again by touch,
that this is the body that was on the cross but is now alive.
Not just a refurbished corpse, but a risen person.

How do we clothe the mystery now?

How can we make the mystery of God real for ourselves
now? I suggest three possible ways, though there are others.
First of all, being aware of the teaching of the Gospel, illus-
trated by the story at the head of this chapter, that what we
do to one another we do to Christ; second, by our deepened
awareness of the sacramental value of creation; and third, by
our use of imagination in our prayer and spiritual lives.

The story with which this chapter started is an example
of a person finding the reality of God in Christ working now
through the hands of one of us. It is a living-out of the precept
contained in the parable of judgement in Matthew 25, the
parable about the sheep and the goats. The parable may fright-
en us with its graphic presentation of judgement by Christ
on the last day; but in positive terms it presents a wonderful
truth – that what we do to one another we do to Christ.

The whole world is sacramental

To the sensibility of the early Celtic Christians, the whole world was sacramental. As we watch water being poured sacramentally on the head of a tiny child, what we see is water, what we hear are human words; yet to the eyes of faith something wonderful is happening, a significance beyond what can be seen, or appreciated by the limits of sense. Water is a clear fluid, translucent, never hiding what lies beneath. Here it is a sign of a spiritual heritage for the child, acknowledging that the world is a casket containing a spiritual treasure; and the child is part of that world, and needs to be nurtured in both body and soul. There is nothing God cannot use to communicate with us; and we, being corporeal, can use only 'things' to communicate with God. The world the Celts could see with the eye and hear with the ear, spoke to them of the Other World, the world of spirit, affirming the mysterious dimension of all reality. The cosmos, nature, history, events, persons, objects, words – everything is capable of carrying the divine energy and life to the receiver. Bread feeds both body and spirit, wine gladdens the heart as it tells of the suffering blood. The earth, the heavens, the body, the spirit, are all wrapped in a cloak of sacrament. The heart bounces back and forth between heaven and earth, God and cosmos, informed and fed, enlivened and dipped in the cup of suffering. Sacraments are the sign language of our life. We are born from the womb and baptized into a community of God's world, and anointed into the loving milieu of the Spirit, we are washed of spiritual disability and fed with the bread of life, we become united body and soul in the unity of love and relationship, are enlisted into a service of word and world, and are finally anointed again for the sacred journey into eternity. Every stage of our journey is marked by sacrament.

The spirit of imagination

Imagination is a wonderful and powerful instrument. It can wander anywhere, not confined by walls. It is an endlessly seeking spirit, which is nonetheless concrete because the pictures it composes are the stuff of the senses (imagined!), the food of endeavour and the power-house of the will.

Imagination is the faculty that forms bridges into, and makes present, the visible and invisible worlds so that they move in and out of each other. The invisible becomes 'tangible' and real in the great arena of one's self. Abstract ideas, general concepts, become particular, concrete happenings and within the sphere of the imagination can be 'touched', 'seen', 'tasted', 'heard' and even 'smelled'. That is why the form of prayer used so often in the *Spiritual Exercises*, called 'Ignatian contemplation' (though he certainly was not the first to use it – it was already several hundred years old when Ignatius commandeered it for the *Exercises*!) is also called 'imaginative contemplation' because it utilizes the imagination as the mechanism by which what is not physically present to us is made so within the imagination. It is a form of prayer that is particularly helpful when considering scenes from the Gospel such as the one you have just been doing, the upper room. We can 'see' the scene in our imagination, we can hear what is said there, the words of Jesus, and others in the scene.

The mediaevals had the belief (according to Boyle in *The Acts of Loyola*) that imagination was so powerful that if a pregnant mother were to see a picture of a monster and it entered her imagination, she would produce a monster! We may not go that far, but nevertheless, the power of imagination is palpable and was instrumental in the change of life in Ignatius himself, as we have seen.

Powers of imagination

When Ignatius began to read the *Lives of the Saints* (*Flos Sanctorum*) and the Gospels (forced upon him, one has to admit, by a household which lacked the imagination to read novels!), that same imagination that had fought battles with the Moors and jousted for the favour of a lady jumped into play again. But this time it enabled him to see himself performing the great ascetic deeds of the saints, now in the service of Christ that he was reading about in the books. These were the images that stuck, that became real, that blossomed into the stream of actions and determinations that were to become his life. His imagination was the nest in which they were hatched.

To see the Christ-mystery

Imagination is a power that gives form to thought. It can put us in contact with situations that reality cannot touch! It is a powerful faculty, and who is to say God is not allowed to use it to fire the spirit? Imaginative prayer was found by Ignatius to be a powerful tool for 'enfleshing the mystery' , and it permeates the *Spiritual Exercises*, not just in the methods of prayer, but also in the descriptions of the parables and contemplations that he proposes for our use. This is especially true of the prayer in the resurrection because the risen Christ is the sum of all the experiences that made him what he is in risen life, namely his life, death and resurrection on earth. So the risen Lord contains all the mysteries we contemplate now. When a mother regards the person of her grown-up son she sees there a whole history, a condensation of the experience of conception, gestation, birth, nurturing and caring that has gone on over a span of years, to arrive at this man now. So the risen Lord, standing before the apostles and his mother in the upper room, sums up the mysteries of his incarnation, life and death into his resurrection. Yet the contemplation is very 'down to earth' as Thomas discovered; but always in these contemplations there is the divinity. When Ignatius speaks of 'composition of place' it is not just inventing a scene (though it is that) but also 'composing myself into the mystery'. It is not just an exercise in imagination but a deep involvement of my whole being and person with the risen Christ in the mystery.

Use your imagination!

There can be a great block to being imaginative in our religion as in our lives. Our lives and religion can be circumscribed by rigid laws and dogmas that cause stagnation. This is particularly true of traditional religion which uses dogma as a fixed point of belief. Eternal verities there must be, but their expression will vary with time.

Furthermore, it is particularly evident today that people themselves change. A person grows and develops, and it is unreal to fix that person at a particular stage of development. We can become fixed at a certain point of development of our faith and refuse to budge further. This happens to groups within the Church that hold to a particular expression of faith as though it is the optimum and only expression, fixed in stone. It denies the developmental quality of creation, and of the life of God in Christ. Let imagination draw us.

Symbols and images

I realize that some traditions do not hold to the use of signs and images; but for others it is a forceful way of bringing a sense of God's presence to the fore. One writer, George MacDonald, in *Defence of Imagination*, goes so far as to see the likeness of human beings to God, not in the intellect or will, but in the imagination as the power giving form and embodiment to thought and aspiration. The human being *bodies forth the thought of God.* Creation itself is an exercise of divine imagination. However, it must be said that we proceed from the love of God as well as from the divine imagination.

Sign of the cross

Imagination was at play when Celtic artists carved the great stone crosses that are to be seen throughout Ireland and Scotland. Besides acting as a sort of spiritual electric fence to protect what they surrounded, they stood as gathering points for Christians, and various ceremonies took place in front of them. The monks of the great monasteries would start to sing their psalms in the church and then form a procession to the place of Golgotha, as the cross itself was termed. The procession then moved round the cross. These images were an expression of deep faith, the carvings representing biblical incidents that taught faith and expressed it. In a very real way they can be seen as enfleshing the mystery of the incarnation.

Christians have always used the cross as a sign of protection, and an expression of faith in Christ's saving power. Celtic monks prayed by extending their arms out to form a cross. It is the sort of gesture that can evoke a sense of God's presence if used with reverence. Try it when you are in a place by yourself.

The sign of the cross was made during various activities of the day to ward off evil and commend the action to God. Adomnan says that if a milk pail in Iona did not have the sign of the cross made over it, a devil might jump in and hide under the milk! The cross stood between the person and all ill-will and mishap.

The icon: true image

In the same way icons have been used to bring the mystery of Christ's incarnation to our attention. The icon has a spirituality within it that invites and draws the user into the reality that is depicted. The painter of the icon regarded the participation of the person looking at it as an essential part of the event depicted in the icon and hoped to draw the beholder into that event. There is a communion between the event or persons represented in the icon and those who contemplate it . . . If you can find an icon that you like, pray using it, remembering that you are being invited into the mystery it expresses.

Did you not, Father God,
feel just a tinge of envy
of the hands of Mary that could clothe
your Son? Or of the breast that fed him?
Yet your desire to be with us
enflesh the mystery of your being,
informing every grain of matter
in our world. Creatures of sense,
we feel, we see, we touch, we taste
your being. And though we did not live
those three explosive years
you walked the earth, we still
can clothe your mystery.
Imagination forms the human
swaddling clothes by which we see,
we touch, and feel; and so
bear witness to you now. And here.

5
To See Anew
The spirit of the senses

Bartimaeus

Bartimaeus (the son of Timaeus) sat by the road begging at the edge of Jericho. He was blind but his sense of hearing was keen. He heard a group of people passing by and learned that it was Jesus of Nazareth with his followers. He began to shout out, 'Jesus, Son of David, please help me!' Many of those near him growled at him, telling him to keep quiet; but this just made him shout louder, 'Son of David, have pity on me!' Jesus heard him, stopped and looked around. 'Call him over here,' he said. So they called him: 'Come on, get up, he's calling you.' Bartimaeus tossed off his cloak, leapt up and went over to Jesus. 'What do you want me to do for you?' asked Jesus. 'Rabbuni, Master, give me back my sight!' Jesus said simply, 'Go along, your faith has saved you.' And Bartimaeus saw again, and followed Jesus along the road.

This cure of Bartimaeus (related in St Mark's Gospel, chapter 10) is not an isolated event. It represents a number of references in the Gospel to 'seeing'. In John 9, particularly, there is a long account of the curing of a blind man by Jesus, much to the chagrin of the Pharisees. For John, such an occurrence is more than simply a cure performed by Jesus, however wonderful that is. It is a sign language indicating how God views creation and its woes. On one occasion Jesus warned his disciples to 'Keep your eyes open . . . have you no perception? Are your minds still closed? Have you got blind eyes, and deaf ears?'

We are so used to our sight that we fail to appreciate it. Only when deprived of it do we realize its potency. A number of people who had been born blind were given sight by a medical operation. Many of them, it was discovered, could not accommodate to this new vision. Some even contemplated suicide because they could not cope.

In this chapter we shall think about trying to see the world and our lives in a new light, or in new ways, some of them already looked at. We shall consider how

1 Seeing anew, glimpsing the mystery, involves a pedagogy of the senses.
2 Discernment helps us to sort out where the sense data are leading.
3 Imagination, sitting with mystery, is a tool for new vision.

New sight

New sight may be external, resulting from a cure of blindness. Or it may be internal, resulting in new ways of seeing life and ourselves. If the new way of seeing is drastic we might call it 'conversion'. Something happens to us that brings us to a threshold of realization, bumps us into a new ball game. Ignatius was heading for a career as a freelance hidalgo when he was laid low by a French cannon-ball on the walls of Pamplona. For him it was a threshold. Lying on his sick-bed he read the only books available, the Gospels and lives of the saints. Gradually his desires changed gear, and his energies began to be channelled into the service of Christ and the kingdom of God.

Changes in life may not be so cataclysmic. Early Celtic society was turned to Christ by the example and preaching of Patrick and others; but the exuberance they felt as a result stands before us in the form of the High Crosses they carved and the intriguing artwork in the *Book of Kells*. The Celtic knot and the spiral took on new meaning: lines that go on and on, as though seeking an end, but never finding one. No beginning, no end – that is, God. Life itself winds endlessly in and out. Emblems and symbols abound in beauty to be seen at many different levels. That exuberance expressed their new sight.

Imagination is new sight

It was all a product of rich imagination in the service of the worship of God. The Celtic artist was not interested in realism. The *Book of Kells* is a textbook of imaginative script, winding spirals coiling in and out of a menagerie of birds and ribbon-snakes endlessly exploring form and pattern and purposeful symbol. The pages writhe with movement and life, the amused playfulness of a monastic scribe. The religion portrayed here is no boring ecclesiastical ritual! Hidden in the patterns are cats eating their own tails, beasts with limbs like strands of chewing gum that pull out into long entwining strings; and of course, wrestling men.

Meister Eckhart, the German mystic, reckoned that we inherit the tremendous creative power of God. Throughout our history the creativity of humankind has been obvious. The power of it has been seen especially in the twentieth century when the human race has seen itself playing with forces beyond its control. We now have the capability of destroying the whole race, of reaching the stars and of reconstructing our bodies and modifying life itself. There is every reason to believe, then, that one of the most godlike traits that we have inherited is that of creativity. The imagination is a proper place to find God. We need to grow more and more into this likeness; like God, we need to create. Yet this is not a sphere which has ever been acknowledged by the Church as more than a decorative adjunct. Beethoven and Michelangelo were never in line for beatification, even though their creativity was truly godlike and a blessing on the world. Artists are the ones in true contact with the beauty of creation, a sacramental contact.

Pedagogy of the senses

Conversion is not an everyday occurrence for us. It is usually a once-in-a-lifetime experience, and depends more on God's life flooding in than our own efforts. Yet we can enhance the quality of our spiritual lives by the proper use of our senses. We need a *pedagogy of the senses* (a phrase used by Michael Ivens, SJ, with reference to the *Spiritual Exercises*). Our senses need to be taught. They are gateways, thresholds between us and the world around; but also between soul and body. They form a bridge, just as imagination is a bridge between notional and concrete reality. And they are the means by which relationship is established. The Celtic Christians recognized 'thresholds', between our world and the 'other' world of spirit which we cannot see. Burial places, for instance, were entry points from our world into the invisible world beyond.

I came across a line in Psalm 84: 'How lovely is your dwelling place, Lord God of hosts.' It meant, not heaven, but the temple. And some of the imagery implied that it was also the natural world. The New English Bible translation of verse 7, 'So they pass on from the outer wall to the inner', referred, I presume, to the temple and progression towards the inner sanctuary; and this reminded me of the movement in our bodily existence from the outer sense data into the inner sanctum of the soul. How lovely is your dwelling place, Lord, this body of mine, and this world we live in! Body and soul are made for each other, and, as in a good marriage, are not complete apart from each other.

Wild horses

The spiritual life will depend on our experience, and that comes in to us via the senses. The senses, however, can become voracious, demanding satisfaction as we stagger from one orgy to another. If the life of the senses is not part of the good of the whole person, then the spiritual life – which concerns the *whole* person – will suffer. The senses lose their fullness, their entry into the soul, their spiritualized, risen form. They become wild horses taking the bit between their teeth and running amok, dragging us along with them. Before we know it, we find ourselves prey to food and drink, to bath salts and television soaps that swamp our eyes and dull our imagination. We become 'sensual' beings, governed by our uncontrolled needs. Paradoxically, if we place our senses in a good relation to our whole being they fall into place in our lives.

There is a need to temper the senses and gear them to the whole, spirit and sense. Spirit wants to express itself *ad extra*, to the world outside, in relationship.

Breaking-in the wild horses

It is because of the 'wild horses' that there is such a strong ascetical tendency in Celtic spirituality, and also in the life of Ignatius. The habit of some Celtic monks of praying for

hours on end standing with arms outstretched in a cold sea
was not an effort to raise money for charity. They were
aware that senses unconnected to the full reality of body
and soul will become uncontrollable. This is the highroad
to addiction which drives to excess and substance abuse.
In the early, over-enthusiastic days of his conversion to God,
Ignatius did set himself ascetical practices to outmatch those
of earlier ascetics; but he later abandoned this competitive
element when he realized that God was probably not
impressed! In fact, nowadays the 'mortification' (or 'killing')
of the senses is not what we would want. Rather we need to
temper them, and help them to take their rightful place in
our body–soul make-up. Isaiah expresses, in the thoughts of
God, a different kind of asceticism. He does not want the
sort of fasting that is external show with no real conversion
of heart:

> Hanging your head like a reed,
> lying down on sackcloth and ashes?
> Is that what you call fasting,
> a day acceptable to Yahweh?

What God wants is a fast from injustice and putting burdens
onto those who are weak.

> to let the oppressed go free,
> and break every yoke,
> to share your bread with the hungry,
> and shelter the homeless poor,
> to clothe the one you see to be naked
> and not turn from your own kin . . .
> Then will your light shine like the dawn
> and your wound be quickly healed over.
>
> (Isaiah 58.4–8)

The senses in the Gospels

Mention of the senses in the Gospels, in various contexts, makes us realize that they are not enemies of our good, but an essential part of it. Being human, Jesus lived a life within the frame of the senses and communicated God's love to others through them, as we ourselves must do.

Vision

Sight is an absorber. Information is conveyed into the mind, where it is processed into action or reaction. But the function of eyes is not only from outside to the inside. They look outwards too, and betray the heart, declaring, I cry, I love, I hate, or simply, I avoid your eye. Eyes are more than mere radar receptors, they are sending messages to whom it may concern.

Our language expresses the inner sense of vision in such expressions as 'I see what you mean' . . . 'Unless I can see the reason I won't go.' Vision is the medium of faith, seeing truth.

'Can't you see? Have you not eyes to see and ears to hear?' Unless you can 'see' you do not believe. For seeing is believing, not with the outward eye, but seeing the meaning beneath the meaning, or the truth between the words. We gain insight: that is *in-sight*, sight within, a new way of seeing life, a change of attitude.

The eye draws us to things, and them to us, a connection, a relationship. Lovers stare deeply into each others' eyes, expressing, simply in the look, their love for each other and their fascination with the mystery of each other's being. When you deeply look at something, it becomes part of you. Try praying by positioning yourself in front of an object, and let it become the centre of your contemplation.

Seeing as God sees

Our hope is to see the world as God sees it. To do that we may need to clean the lenses of the eyes. But how does God see the world? Ignatius, in a meditation, imagined the Trinity gazing down on the world, watching people going helter skelter for hell and damnation – a somewhat pessimistic view, but often approximating to what seems to be happening in our world! If we see it with more optimistic eyes we know it for the place where the Holy Spirit is active, making it the playground of God! Not a very serious or theological thought? Well, if God, as some say, *played* in creation, and he is still active in creation, then it is his playground, the focus of his creativity and imagination.

The oil painting

Spend time before an object, a vase perhaps or a painting that you admire, and simply absorb it. Let your body be still, only the eyes moving. I once stood contemplating a large oil painting of a vase of flowers:

> As I gaze a chord is struck within me,
> the Go-Between Spirit fills my sense
> in mutual recognition! I enter in,
> I now become the picture, my spirit
> wrapped in this material thing.
> Artist, wherever you are, whoever you are,
> I embrace you in your creation,
> I recognize you in what you have evoked.
> I glory, through this paint,
> in the fabric of your being.

I then gazed at a tree with the same intensity:

And as I gaze at the tree, staying
with the details of its form, I sense,
behind the work, the Artist of Creation.

We may become so familiar with our surroundings that we no longer 'see' them. We can assume we see things, what they are like. But often we see how we expect to see, we predetermine the world around us. So the disciples 'failed' to see Jesus on the road to Emmaus until he broke the bread; and Mary Magdalene failed to see him as the gardener. We too can 'fail' to see Jesus in one another.

In Matthew 6 Jesus refers to the eye as a kind of lamp for the whole body. Just as a light can be dulled if the glass is not clean, so your eye has to be 'clean' in order to fill you with light. Again, if there is a disease in the eye you cannot see and your whole body is affected. You are in darkness. There is this constant interplay, in the Gospels, between physical seeing and seeing with the heart and soul. That is how we need to read Scripture, with heart and soul as well as the eye. It has been said that only a contemplative reading of the Gospels brings you to the glory of God in Jesus Christ.

So, ask yourself: How do I look at the world and people? With love, or as threat? We need to train our eyes to see, and our hearts to make the transition to the inner sense of sight, so that we can see the invisible in the visible.

Touch

Touch creates contact, flesh to flesh, hand to hand. And the message is conveyed, of force, or love, or even casual indifference. Touch conveys relationship. It is the essence of our bodiliness. By it we communicate directly, whether in friendship when we shake hands, or in anger when we strike another, or in love when we embrace. We gesture with our hands to express ourselves.

Touch seemed to be significant for Jesus in terms of power. He knew when the woman with the haemorrhage touched even his clothes, because power had gone out of him. He used touch in some of the healing miracles, such as the healing of the deaf man in Mark 7.32–7: A man was brought to Jesus who was deaf and dumb. The people asked him to lay his hands on the man to cure him. Jesus led the man away from the crowd of people. Then he put his fingers into the ears of the man, put a little spittle on his tongue. Then he prayed, looking up to heaven, sighed and said, 'Ephphatha!' which means 'Be opened!' The man's tongue was set loose, and his ears were cleared, and he could speak and hear.

Touch expresses intimacy. Jesus defended the woman who had bathed his feet in her tears and dried them with her hair, and then kept kissing his feet and perfuming them. For a man so at ease with touch, even of such a demonstrative kind, his saying to Mary Magdalene, after his resurrection, 'Do not touch me' seems a little odd, and has been translated and explained in various ways. For, later in the upper room when he appeared there, Jesus invited Thomas to put his finger in the nail-holes in his hands, and his hand in the wound in his side.

The inner sense of touch is familiar to us. We talk about being 'touched' when we are presented with a present on our birthday. Prayer, we hope, will touch us, or move us, in our hearts and in our lives.

How do we train our sense of touch? Sometimes by deprivation, or being willing to subject our body to something other than sheer comfort, not for the sake of discomfort, but because any training requires restraint. But also by being more aware of textures, and by expressing our care and concern by that sense. A woman working at the checkout desk of a store was asked, as an experiment, to touch the

arm of some of the people she was checking out. The cus-
tomers were then asked whether or not the woman at the
desk had smiled when dealing with them. Those who had
been 'touched' said she had, those who were not touched
said she had not smiled – even though she had not, in fact,
smiled at all! The touch had conveyed the smile!

In prayer, try using your hands to express your desire, or
your emotion. To express your sorrow before God, and
asking for his mercy, hold your fists clenched, and slowly
open them out until they are extended with palms upwards
in an attitude of receiving.

Taste

Taste is a testing ground and a place of appreciation. The
chemical receptors discern taste.

The film *Babette's Feast* made a deep impression on me.
Yet a large part of it was given over to the preparation and
cooking of a great dinner of a most elaborate kind, by a
dedicated cook. The outcome of the meal was the uniting
of a religious community which was falling apart. It is
reminiscent of the 'messianic banquet' in Isaiah:

> On this mountain Yahweh will prepare for all peoples a
> banquet of rich food, a banquet of fine wines, of food rich
> and juicy, of fine strained wines . . . The Lord Yahweh will
> wipe away the tears from every cheek.
>
> (Isaiah 25.6, 8a)

The symbolism of the Eucharist is evident. Christ chose to
remind us of his presence in the form of the bread and wine
of communion, the sign of unity.

Like anything else, food improperly used can become the
means of sin and abuse. Gluttony has been a form of abuse

of the sense of taste as long as history is recorded. Roman orgies were frightening in their deliberate lack of control in the matter of food; while in our own day drink and drugs are in the same category. Eating too fast can result in not actually tasting the food at all. Take a piece of bread and chew it very slowly, being aware of the taste and letting it convey to you the benefit of the food we are lucky enough to have; and pray for those who are starving.

Speech

Speech goes along with taste as involving the tongue. Returning late one evening on the train from Edinburgh to Glasgow I had the misfortune to be sitting just behind three youths draped over the seats like Drake in his hammock (but not, alas, a thousand miles away!) and conducting a very loud conversation which consisted of a few items of information strung together with 'f's. The f*** word functioned as noun, verb, pronoun, adverb and conjunction. It seemed to be the only adjective in the language. It acted as exclamation mark and something to breathe in with. Our poor unfortunate language was limping around like a plucked chicken with only one feather left. And yet, speech can be so gracious, conveying inspiration as well as information. Make a point of saying things carefully, so that your tongue gives glory to God, and upholds the person you are speaking to.

Smell

Smell is a wild and woolly thing, often sensed in whiffs and sniffs that nevertheless can convey strong messages. We are not in the same league as the common dog when it comes to smell! When we go out to admire the view, the dog goes out to admire the smell. Yet even for us, smell is a powerful sense, and can summon up memory like a geni from a lamp. I've mentioned how the whiff of turf burning in the Hebrides brought back a whole world of my childhood in Ireland.

Smell is carried into us on the breath, and breath in the Bible is evoked by Spirit. Be still and breathe in, recognizing that you breathe in the Spirit, the life of God. It seems strange to talk of educating the sense of smell; yet we can become more aware of it. Go out into the fields, or into the street, stop still and simply become aware of the different scents that are being wafted to you.

John's Gospel, at chapter 12.3, describes how Mary took a whole pint of very expensive perfume made of pure nard, poured it over Jesus' feet, and wiped them with her hair. 'The sweet smell of the perfume pervaded the house.' The scent was obviously too much for Judas who was too conscious of the price of perfume rather than the significance of the love carried by the gesture.

Listening

'Listen, you who have ears to hear,' said Jesus. The art of listening is an essential part of spiritual direction. It is not only listening to the sound, the words, but also to the silences, to what is *not* said. God, speaking through the poet Rilke, likens himself to the rest between two notes which, if they are sounded together, are discordant.

Like the other senses, listening has become blunted in our modern life, by excess, by the need for instant satisfaction. Many people use music, for example, as background noise. To listen to music one must not be doing anything else. Much music nowadays is composed (or perhaps run off the computer!) to be used as 'mood music' which does not require real attention but is used like bath salts or 'air freshener'. The effect of music can be dynamic. It carries the spirit of energy, or of peace, of relationship, of expression.

The Celts listened to nature, and this is obvious from the poetry they wrote as a result. And so they heard the voices of nature:

> The talk of the rushes has come . . .
> Loud melody enriches the hill
> The stuttering quagmire prattles
> . . . a brawling white stream . . .
> (from 'Finn's Poem on Mayday', in
> Mary Low, *Celtic Christianity and
> Nature*, p. 122)

This listening requires utter stillness, and quieting of the restlessness we often succumb to. Try listening with total attention. Be still and listen to sounds around you with such total commitment that the moment your attention strays, the moment you start 'thinking' rather than listening, switch it back to listening. It is very simple, and very difficult. How long can you keep it up?

Again, try listening to a piece of music with total attention, not as background noise, but with the attention you would pay to a sound in the hall when you think it could be a burglar!

Ignatius listening

One of the things Ignatius was good at was noticing what went on inside him. As he lay on his couch whiling away the hours as his leg grew strong again, he daydreamed about his quest to win the attention of a high-born lady. But then his attention would switch to thinking about deeds he could do in the service of Christ, a new sort of king. He began to realize that the two sorts of daydreaming affected him in two different ways. The lady fired his imagination and his romantic aspirations but left him dry and discontented afterwards; whereas the thoughts of serving Christ not only fired his imagination at the time, but left him stronger, more resolute, confirmed. From this he realized that God can call us by drawing us from deep within ourselves, moving our desires towards himself. From this rather modest beginning Ignatius formulated what has come to be called (rather grandly!) 'discernment of spirits'.

We are moved, hither and thither, by different 'spirits' – nudges towards or away from what is right and godly. If we are aware of what is 'good spirit' and what is bad we can choose what is positive in our lives and not just be blown around by the wind of fortune. Our desires are not clear-cut. There is a mound of rubbish cluttering up our judgement. Most of discernment is 'clearing the decks' of the junk so that we can see what will be for our good. I remember one of those astonishing nature programmes on TV (how do they *get* those pictures?) of a chameleon, clambering along the branch of a tree, eyes rolling around, and flicking out its tongue to snap up a huge spider off its web. Then it stood there, eyes rolling around with the legs of the spider sticking out of its mouth at all angles, before gulping it down.

Chameleons?

Isn't that just us, so often? Looking around for distractions, eyes in all directions, seeking tasty morsels to titillate our palate, or things to comfort us. And what we find is often enough a sort of spider! Our colour changes with the passing fashion or peer-pressure, or because the advertisements tell us what colour we should be. Pardon me, chameleon, I'm just using you as a symbol of our uncentred, distracted selves!

The need in me is to find out who I am in myself and to stand within that place, irrespective of what the publicity declares I must have for my happiness. That place is one of strength. It is where the real person stands, like John the Baptist – not a 'reed swaying in the breeze' wafted around by the wind of change – and where Jesus himself stood. Both of them suffered for it, of course. It is not necessarily an easy place to be, a place of mockery and isolation for some.

The awareness of what is 'right' for us is a product of both body and spirit, an awareness of what is moving us in our lives, and where it is leading us. Seeing anew involves this discernment, this attempt to see with the eye of God within our own selves and to take decisions and direction in that way.

Ignatius and the 'Other World'

At the time of Ignatius there was a general belief in the Other World, that of angels and spirits, both good and bad. In a meditation called the 'Two standards' he represents a battle between good, in the person of Christ, and evil, in the person of Satan. All the details are symbolically pointed: Christ is placed on a plain outside Jerusalem, city of peace, while Satan, described as the enemy of our race, is seated outside Babylon, the city of confusion. While Christ summons people to follow him and help in the conversion of the world, Satan summons demons to help in the opposite direction.

That is the story as Ignatius saw it, in his imagination. It was a reality that he firmly believed, the reality of powers and dominations at work in the world, some working for good, others for evil, two opposed forces. The Other World was, then, a reality for Ignatius and influenced the way he prayed, thought and acted.

Other World

In our day, the belief in otherworldly reality has been eroded. Perhaps this is the result of our scientific training, what cannot be seen and measured does not exist! It is like stopping breathing because one cannot see the air. Although belief in the Other World may sometimes be a source of superstitious practice, it is also a source of faith and energy if rightly perceived.

The sense of wonder is a natural instrument for enhancing our imaginative lives. It is an opening of the senses to what is before our eyes and allowing imagination to fill in what underlies it. Wonder is particularly important in imaginative contemplation. Allow wonder to give rise to wondering, to rumination. Why is this thus?

Some have seen creativity as a way in which our image of God, the mould in which we are designed, is particularly in evidence. Creation is a product of God's imagination, and we are a product of his love and imagination. The creativity of the Celts and Ignatius gave rise to a dynamic faith filled with awe, determination, energy and sheer delight. These are attributes which do not strike us as redolent of our churches today, in many cases.

Beyond appearances

The Celts had a way of seeing behind the appearances of things, seeing the 'mountain behind the mountain', seeing at the horizon's edge the light of other worlds. Through this ability to imagine what was really there but could not be seen by the physical eye they recognized the spirit-world of the Bible. The angels are invoked again and again in their prayers:

God, give charge to Thy blessed angels
To keep guard around this stead tonight,
A band sacred, strong and steadfast,
That will shield this soul-shrine from harm.
(from Oliver Davies and Fiona Bowie,
Celtic Christian Spirituality, p. 99)

The Celtic 'Other World'

The Celtic belief is to be found expressed in a modern poem, 'O world invisible', in which Francis Thompson speaks of seeing the invisible, touching the intangible and knowing the unknowable Other World. The poem asks for an awareness of that other sphere, showing that by the use of imagination we can encounter that world and experience the

traffic of Jacob's ladder
Pitched between heaven and Charing Cross.

and witness Christ's walking on the water

Not of Gennesareth, but Thames!

Called to widen our horizons
and view the old
with eyes that are new,
we see created mystery
and a world behind our world.
Alas! The pathways of perception
are cluttered, the gates rusty,
piled high with rubbish.

Our senses,
those throughways to creation,
must needs be cleansed,
must learn again to see
pure light, to discern pure scent,
to feel the texture of God
and savour the subtle taste
of heavenly food.

Deep down,
reaching into the very
Ground of our Being,
the compass of right and wrong,
good and bad. And our choices
reach up through the sense,
through our sight, touch, hearing,
smell and taste, out into the world.
They are the channels through which
we receive the gifts of creation.

As these riches enter the body
they are transposed into soul-gifts.
We see with new eyes, touch
the goodness of God, hear divine
resonances, smell fragrance beyond
the scent that enters.

By these channels
we are enabled to communicate
the love of God. They are the strings
that make the puppet dance, the very
means of relationship. We gaze at
one another, communicate
gently by touch, express the depths of soul
by the speech of our mouths, we hear
each other's heart-beats, as John heard
the heart of Jesus, beating for us.

6
Immanent Love
Love, the glue of creation

> And Jacob lay his head on a stone and slept.
> And waking from his dream he said: Surely
> Yahweh is in this place and I never knew it.
> (Genesis 28)

Truly, God is in this place
Truly, God is in this place
God is in this place
God is in this
God is.

But if God is in this place why can I not see him?

Eyes desiring only the glitter of distraction are blind.
Ears deadened by clamour and lies are deaf.
Hands shielded from the touch of the earth are numb.
Listen and hear, Look and see, Touch and be touched.

God is where he acts. Where love is shown, God is there.
Love, finally, is all that matters.

1 We look to the God who is present in our world.
2 This enables us to 'find God in all things' in our world.
3 God is the unifying force of creation, and hence of the
   human race.

God here, and God there

You might say that God is here, there, and everywhere. When people first began to describe God in Christian terms they stressed how 'removed' he was from human experience and our world. He is totally *other*. But at the same time he is the God of creation, totally involved with it, as attentive to it as a footballer is to the ball at his feet. The very fact that God can be both of those things, totally other (the word they used was 'transcendent') and totally present and involved (and the word they used for this was 'immanent') points to the fact that God is not able to be described in our terms. God is mystery. And since he is present in our world it means that the earth itself is mysterious. Science is finding out more and more about the universe, and will go on finding out more and more because the mystery is like an ocean without a bottom – no matter how deep you go you do not compass the whole thing.

God is an emptying sort of love

Love suffers from being regarded as a soap-opera mixture of sex, pop-songs and cuddly feelings. In fact, it is a much sturdier animal altogether, as you might suspect since it stems from God. It is about giving oneself. That is what God does: each person of the Trinity gives to the others, goes out of self to the other. The love we celebrate in life, in song, is a reflection of this. The stress in our day on the self and self-fulfilment, tends to centre love on our own gain.

God *gave* in creation because it is his nature. When Jesus came on earth he emptied himself, gave himself to us as St Paul says. Our love will not be authentic unless it is a giving to another. If we receive love back, so much the better, but the essential thing is the giving. That is why the crucifixion is the final, conclusive sign of God's love, the total emptying out of himself which Christ experienced on the cross. As the Taizé song says: *Ubi caritas et amor, ibi Deus est.* Where there is love and loving-kindness, God is there. St John says this clearly in a letter: 'Dear friends, let us love each other because love comes from God. If you love you are a child of God and know God. If you don't love, you don't know God, because God is love.' His followers grew a bit tired of his constant repetition of 'God is love', 'Love one another', and they asked if he had anything new to say. But that simple message was enough for him.

It was enough, too, for the Celtic Christians. They relied mainly on St John because of his tendency to mystery and his emphasis on love. These two things are related: mystery and love. A poet said that love's function is to fabricate unknownness. Love and mystery are connected.

Creation as mystery

God is mystery, and creation takes the mysterious element from its source in God. That mystery was what 'scared' Jacob when he realized that God was present. Perhaps it is no coincidence that 'scared' is an anagram for 'sacred'! He whispered: 'This is nothing less than a house of God; this is the gate of heaven!' The sacred, the 'numinous' as Rudolf Otto calls it, causes reverential awe so that the hairs on the back of your neck stand up.

Mircea Eliade described poetically the difference between the religious outlook on the world and that of the non-religious person. Nature, for the former, is always instinct with a religious value. The cosmos is a divine creation and hence sacred. This is recognizable in the very structure of the world. As the religious person contemplates the world he or she discovers what Eliade calls the *many modalities of the sacred* and thus of being. The sacred quality shines through creation, which is transparent to it.

Thin places

Jacob named the place of his dream 'Bethel', the House of God. Yet it was a place here on earth. This is a reminder that there are special places where the presence of God or of the spirit world is palpable. They are referred to sometimes as 'thin places', where the veil separating this from the other world seems to be very thin, like a very fine silk which is translucent. For the Celts, cemeteries were 'thin places', since they were a passage from this world into the next. The world of spirits, waiting to be found, does not impose itself or force us to see. Ruins in Celtic lands were often regarded, not as empty shells, but full of presences, and stories were told of men who refused to sell land for development because the ruins of the house where their ancestors lived, and their spirits still inhabited, were present in the field. Places where there had been some manifestation of God's presence, such as the burning bush in Exodus, where Moses experienced the presence of God, and the Mount Horeb of Elijah, retained a sacred quality. Centres of worship are recognized as numinous, as places where God's presence becomes manifest. This was a familiar fact from the Bible, where God made himself felt by the cloud that descended on the tabernacle in the wilderness, and later came down into the Holy of Holies in the temple.

The beyond: glimpses of mystery

The world we belong to is not confined to what we can see and touch. It may be that our scientific upbringing will have led us to believe that only what is measurable and visible is real. Thus have we been led, unimaginatively, up a garden path without wonder and mystery. Or rather, where there is mystery (look up to the stars, look down into the depths of the ocean, to *The Blue Planet*, to a coral reef . . .), we feel opened out to a totally larger reality. Do you ever have moments of ecstasy when your whole being is elevated? When you hear music that appeals to you? When you make love? When you stand on a cliff on a breezy day overlooking the sea?

The Centre for Religious Experience started by Alister Hardy in Oxford in 1969 (and now renamed, after him, the 'Alister Hardy Research Centre') has done a survey of the occurrence of religious experience among ordinary people. The survey discovered, surprisingly, that in a wide sample of the population, 70 per cent have had some sort of religious experience. Few of them have ever related their experience to others since they are shy of talking about such matters, feeling that they would not be believed, or if they were, that they would be considered 'odd'. They would not, of course, be odd at all! There is a God within us that responds to the God out there.

Those moments of uplift!

The poet Kathleen Raine talks of being aware of 'paradise descending in the morning sun'. Most of us, at one time or another, will have such moments. Our spirits are raised up and we become more aware of the goodness of God. There have been moments when listening to music that I have found my heart in my throat and my spirit uplifted by a change of key or the striking of open strings. The Jesuit who trained us compared heaven to such a moment which is then prolonged into eternity! I can remember times, too, when walking in the hills, being suddenly and unexpectedly delighted by a view, the unexpectedness giving it a 'gift' quality. Walking one day with a companion on a long hill in the Lake District enveloped in a mist and progressing cautiously because we knew we were near the edge, the mist suddenly cleared enough to reveal a glimpse of a whole landscape, a whole world! Way down below us. A glimpse of an unknown wonderland!

I am sure you will yourself have similar moments to recount. Not moments of ecstasy, you may say. But they are tinges of something 'beyond' that we momentarily experience.

A contemplation to deepen love

St Ignatius seemed to have many such moments. Staring into a river, gazing up at the stars, and just when praying in his room, he could sense deeply the presence of something sacred. He wrote a prayer to help put us in the frame of mind to allow such a sense to be given to us. He called it 'A contemplation for love' and I want to look at it in detail. It shows us a man given over completely to the awareness of God and Jesus. It expresses a spirit of thanksgiving for the gifts of creation, for a deep sense of God present in creation and for a sense of the 'labour' and suffering involved in it. It is from this contemplation that the expression 'finding God in all things' takes its origin. The wonder of God's presence and action was to be found in the commonplace, the everyday, the mystery of the obvious. It has been said that only the trivial mind needs the reassurance of supernatural events, since it cannot see that everything, *every*thing, in the world around is pure miracle. Ignatius could see, and wanted everyone to see, the depth of God's presence in everything.

Doing, not reading and thinking

To describe the 'Contemplation for love' in cold print is to suffer from the same disadvantage as staring at a skeleton as a way of seeing a living person. The writer was more interested in 'doing' than 'reading'. The statements are terse and pragmatic to the ear. In fact this contemplation, as stated in the book, is the bare bones of a great love poem between ourselves, God and nature. But the poem is composed, the skeleton must be enfleshed, from within the heart and soul of the person contemplating.

Coming from a man of action as well as contemplation, love is a *doing*. We are confronted by the need to take responsibility, the need for commitment. Put your money where your mouth is. Give yourself, share yourself. In marriage, it is the giving of self to the spouse; in everybody, it is the gift of self to God. But the giving is mutual, and God is the source of everything. What can you give to someone who is the source of everything? All we can give is ourselves, our love. These two notes show that we are in the realms of love in this prayer. Creation is an expression of God's love, and in the midst of creation we can find God and God's love present. But if the love is to be mutual then creation must respond to that love of God.

Heaven is *for* you

In our spiritual life one of the hardest commodities to find is real encouragement. We don't seem to encourage each other enough in the things that are deepest to our life in God. So it is refreshing, at the beginning of this contemplation, to find what is called a 'Composition of place', that is, a setting, an entrée to the prayer, an entering into its spirit, body and soul. It seems, at first sight, like a bit of a frolic: being aware of what we know to be the fact, that the whole court of heaven, angels, saints, and those loved ones who have gone before us, and of course the Trinity, are there for us.

Lest anyone should feel that this is a formidable and forbidding (and judging) array, we are left in no doubt that this multitude is rooting for us, wanting to help and encourage us. To know that God and his whole entourage in heaven are standing on the terraces roaring in our support can do us no end of good. For we do often think that God is eyeing us like a CCTV camera waiting for us to steal something off the shelves. But, no, he is for us, and if God is for us, who can be against?

As already noted, such an awareness of the court of heaven is quite natural for the Celtic spirit. God is in no way an absentee landlord, making himself known only when he wants to collect rent money. He is more like a part of the family. In fact, there is a similarity in the attitude of the Celt and Ignatius towards the Lord of all things: an attitude of both reverence and familiarity. Where familiarity is truly based on love, it is reverential.

The God within

Having given ourselves this fair wind in our sails, we move into the main body of the prayer which is trying to deepen our awareness of the relationship of God to creation. For, although Ignatius was well aware of the awesomeness of a God who is above and beyond this world, he also finds God present in and throughout creation.

Eternally thankful

To be thankful is a factor which makes the difference between a sombre, off-white life, and a glowing one. Think how you feel when a friend is forever telling you how awful life is! You begin not to want to phone them any more. In fact, we have so much to be thankful for!

'Remember', says the prayer, 'all the benefits of God, of creation, of salvation and how I myself have been gifted.' *Remember*. Memory constitutes us, plants and roots us. It places us firmly in the context of our whole life. Those events, places, people that were dear to us are not lost: they are the forces that have brought us to where we are. To us, time-bound as we are, these things seem to have floated away and become lost. To God all is present.

Memories may be painful. By remembering, we can bring them to the Lord to the altar of healing.

Memory is a prime factor in Ignatian spirituality. He strongly advocated a prayer of remembrance of the past day or week or whatever period we wish to recall.

Memory reminds us what our experience has been. However, the facts of the past are useful only if reflected upon, in order, first of all, to be thankful for them, but more important, to learn from them.

Recall all the gifts of God for you, of creation, of redemption, and all your own personal gifts. Spend time doing this, recalling everything you can think of. Pay special attention to your own personal gifts, without being shy about them, and thank God for them, using, if you wish, the prayer of the Magnificat (Luke 1.46–55). These gifts may be yours, but they are God's gifts to you!

Celtic memories

The Celts were part of an oral society. Their histories, embroidered with imagination, were recited by the bards and poets and woven into the fabric of their lives. In the Christian era the monks took over their role, reciting the stories of the Bible and salvation history. These things were written down in the manuscripts and on the High Crosses. Memory is of crucial importance to any Christian. But Ignatius is asking us to make it a personal history too, our own gifts, graces and salvation.

God in everything created

The second section of the prayer is to see how God dwells in creatures. The outlook of Ignatius coincides exactly with the Celts in this. The Celtic theologian and writer Pelagius could well have been describing the same point when he wrote:

Look at the animals roaming the forest: God's spirit dwells within them. Look at the birds flying across the sky: God's spirit dwells within them. Look at the tiny insects crawling in the grass: God's spirit dwells within them. Look at the fish in the river and sea: God's spirit dwells within them. There is no creature on earth in whom God is absent . . . his breath has brought every creature to life. Look too at the great trees of the forest; look at the wild flowers and the grass in the fields; look even at your crops. God's spirit is present within all plants as well. The presence of God's spirit in all living things is what makes them beautiful; and if we look with God's eyes, nothing on the earth is ugly.

(quoted in J. Philip Newell, *Listening for the Heartbeat of God*, pp. 10, 11)

One of Ignatius' great heroes was St Francis of Assisi, and that may well have been the source and inspiration for this part of the prayer. Whatever its origin, it brings God into the very life of our senses, enabling us to see and feel his presence in blades of grass and the sound of the wind crossing a wheatfield. And in the stillness within nature. God comes to us in and through creation, not apart from it. This is Ignatius' Song of Songs for the earth and God's creation, truly his Song of the Earth. But it is not spelled out in his words, but is issued as an invitation to us to pray it. More than that, it will become our way of looking at nature and seeing God's Spirit everywhere at work in it. Our culture is estranged from the earth, and from a relationship of mutuality, and so does not come to understand the wisdom contained in the wonder and sanctity of a landscape, even a wild one. Hopkins, the Jesuit poet, wrote:

> The world is charged with the grandeur of God,
> It will flame out like shining from shook foil
> It gathers to a greatness like the ooze of oil
> Crushed . . .
>
> ('God's Grandeur')

What is to be gained from encouraging this sense of God present in the earth and all elements?

For the spiritual person it is, of course, an expression of a reality which cannot be seen, but is nevertheless real. The person standing in the sunshine on a glorious summer day, as described, for instance, in 'Hebridean altars', feels the need to praise the sun-blessed day as a jewel dropped from God's hand. Such a beautiful day must have come from a beautiful mind. The watcher is influenced by this experience so as to make his life itself more given to beauty and right doing and self-giving.

God's Spirit is within us, and we can have reference to the Spirit to guide us.

Nature's church

The search is on, these days, for the 'church without walls'. St Patrick described how he discovered his faith when outdoors, working as a shepherd in the woods and mountains. 'I used to rise to pray, through snow, through frost, through rain . . .' (*Confession*). And when he had to explain the faith to two princesses, daughters of a pagan king, he talked of a God who is present in both heaven and earth and in all things in them, quickening and supporting.

One of the great attractions nowadays of Celtic spirituality is its attitude to creation. Our Celtic hermit (we read) wants his own little shed in a remote place, next to a wood, plenty of birds, a pool of water where he no doubt did his washing but talked of washing away his sins!

Well, who wouldn't wish for that! It could come straight out of a Travel Guide. Yet it does reveal the Celtic love of nature; and going along with that, an eye that notices the details of the surroundings. The hermit delights in watching Pangur, his cat, stalk a mouse, as he himself stalks words to put on his page. It is the same eye for minute detail that is seen in the decorations of the pages of the *Book of Kells*, alive with animal life. 'Pleasant is the glittering of the sun today upon these margins because it flickers so!' – scribbled by a scribe in an idle moment on the margin of a volume of Cassiodorus that he was copying.

The Celtic saint was part of his landscape, not an intruder, nor an owner, not an exploiter. His ambition was not to stand out from the surroundings, not to be a 'sore thumb' in the picture. In fact, he may not even have wished to be in the foreground at all, the central figure. He wanted to fade into the scenery like a green knoll in a landscape of grass or a rock among crags. Only in this way could he absorb the real life of nature. The animal knows, with the accumulated wisdom of thousands of years of evolution, that if he be prey he must camouflage his presence. The saint was not 'prey' except to the aggression of the terrain. But to exist in the fierce landscape of his choice he had to become part of it, and present a smooth surface to the attacks of the biting wind or the gouging sea.

Mary Low, in *Celtic Christianity and Nature*, points out that many early poems like 'Cetamon' and 'My tidings for you', don't actually make reference to religious things; but they show what she calls *a primal sense of kinship* with nature that gives them a sense of the power of God who is present, on which we depend for our happiness and survival. The close observation of nature, with the wonder that ensues, is itself a religious act.

Promoting the good

That would immediately appeal to the pagan hearers, because they too believed that creation was good. They were brought up to regard the earth as sacred and to experience the holiness of the cosmos. Elsewhere in the Church, pagan things were regarded as evil and to be destroyed. Great energy was used in fulminating against the natural world, cutting down sacred trees, and despoiling sacred wells. Spirit was exalted over matter, heaven over earth and a wedge was driven between human nature and the rest of creation. The Celtic Church did not do this, but accepted what went before it and blessed and baptized it rather than condemning and destroying it. St Samson in Cornwall, coming across a group of heathens dancing round their sacred stones, and finding them amenable to the Christian faith, drew a cross on the stones and then joined in the dance!

In recent years there has been an enlightening reversal of the destructive tendencies of much evangelization. We are so familiar with the heart-shrinking tales of the effect of missions on many native populations, abolishing their customs and substituting practices that were not essential to the message of the gospel but were Western ways of thinking. So many babies emptied out with the bathwater!

In one of the General Congregations of the Jesuit Order in recent years a document expressed the conviction that God's Spirit is operative everywhere in the world, and not just in the Church as visible; and so when a missionary goes to another land he or she does not now presume to carry the truth to that people, but comes to find Christ and the Spirit at work there and help to make it explicit. Were we to stop there, seeing creation as all things bright and beautiful, we might be accused of ignoring the true picture of a suffering world. It is an accusation that has been levelled at me after talking about the Celtic appreciation of nature.

The labouring God

The third section of the 'Contemplation for love' gives a rather different slant on God's presence. God is now represented as one who is present in suffering and the labour of the earth, always at work for me in all created things. What is indicated here is not a static reality, but a dynamic one, and one which goes on now. The supposed reply of Eckhart to one asking what God did all day ('She lies on a bed giving birth!') seems over-stark and startling, but expresses an aspect of the labouring creator. God's entering into the toils of life has been likened to a mother labouring in childbirth. Creation is indeed a labour of love. God works and suffers. This came to its fullness in the life and death of Christ, who showed us God present in our whole wrangling and striving existence, and who accepted the suffering that we are burdened with.

My childhood idea of God creating the cosmos, like a magician producing a rabbit out of a hat, is replaced here by a concept of creation as a *labour*, 'love's austere and lonely offices', as the poet says. But creation was not like the labours of Hercules that, once completed, he sat back; it is something continuing, now, forever. The divine potter is still at work.

Tagore says to one praying in church that God is out where the tiller is breaking up the hard ground, present in sun and showers, and in the dust!

Can this image be found in Celtic spirituality? Only, I think, in the sense of a God who is involved in humanity, lock, stock and barrel; the rough with the smooth, the suffering along with the happy periods. A psalter from the ninth or tenth century (*Saltair na Rann*), written by Oengus the Culdee, a hermit, gives a description of God as king, actively, physically making the world, forming, fashioning, hewing it out. The labouring and suffering God is seen clearly in the person of Jesus, who gives himself for us.

The endless source

God is the endless source. In the last part of Ignatius' prayer, God's action is compared to the rays of the sun pouring down, never being diminished by the giving. This is an image coming out of the storehouse of Ignatius' Trinitarian prayer. Everything comes from above, from the Father of Light. It recalls how, at Manresa, Ignatius had a vision of God creating the world, and he saw it as rays of light streaming from a source of light. Later on, he saw Christ many times as the sun.

Celtic life-giving sun

The imagery is close to that of the early Celts. The sun, provider of light and life, was given attention that was practically worship. The phenomenon of the sun dancing at Easter sunrise was a statement about the resurrection.

The fountain too represents a source which is unending, constantly pouring out with great abundance, the water of life. Water represents the Spirit. Again, we are reminded of a vision of Ignatius, sitting by the river Cardoner, an enlightenment which he could never quite explain.

Both of these images, of the rays of the sun and the stream of water from the fountain, are reminders of the constancy of the source of God's life and grace. God's life is always there for us, whether or not we are taking advantage of its availability.

A God of unity, a God of history

If God is the source of all creation and his Spirit breathes through the world, then we have to conclude, first, that all of humankind are one, at the deepest possible level; and, second, that God is to be found in our history and in the movements of our times. What I am pointing to are ideals. Humankind is not united, and the movements of our times are by no means all good. But maybe we should pay attention to the ideals.

Unity within creation

Our common origin in God gives a unity to all parts of creation. The Russian writer Solovyev had a vision of humanity as one. It is a perspective badly needed in our world today, where conflicting forces are likely to demolish our earth. The events of 11 September 2001, when the World Trade Center was demolished in Manhattan, brought this home to us. We cannot solve our differences by bombs and war. Force and world domination are dangerous toys to play with. Will the world ever be able to accept Christ's command, 'love your enemies'?

We are unified at root, by our common humanity, and our origin in a God who is at work within life – helping, raising it, giving it an impulse to drive it. He is found at the heart of all matter, and at the heart of my being. I am immersed in God's creative action. I bless the vicissitudes, good and bad fortune, my own character, virtues and faults. The bosom of Mother Earth is in some way the bosom of God.

Recent events have forced us to ask the question: 'How do you handle difference between people in such a way as to avoid conflict and violence?' Our total lack of success to do this over the last centuries would make it seem impossible to reconcile differences. Is it a matter of smoothing out the differences? To expect that is to ask for something impossible as well as undesirable. To be all the same would curb God's creative variety. Do we really want to be a set of scientific clones?

Relationship is with the 'other'. It has its meaning in the difference between us. Any true relationship cannot rely – does not want to rely – on total similarity of desire and need. There has to be give and take, the acceptance of things that we ourselves find difficult. Only in this attempt to meet the other, to understand his or her needs and attitudes, can real love lie.

God of history

The God present in our earth is present in the movements of history, in the patterns of human living, in the desires of humankind. There are two ways of seeing this: that God's Spirit is to be located within the movements of our times, and that God can, and does, bring good out of evil and sin.

The Spirit is to be found working in the happenings of our world, in our endeavours, within the change that is inevitable in our world and society. It is of the essence of matter to change. As Christians our calling is to monitor such change in the light of the gospel, and to strengthen and support movements where we can discern the presence of the Spirit of God. That discernment will also see where the Spirit of God is being opposed, and where that is clear, we will challenge.

For this discernment to be effective, and true to God's Spirit, we have to be balanced and free from the prejudices that normally hold us. Care is needed to make sure that we are not condemning change simply because something is new and different from the old. Our tendency is to stick at a certain point in our history, and proclaim anything beyond that to be wrong. Our challenge is to discern prayerfully where God's Spirit is guiding us, as he or she guided the people of Israel in the desert. Jesus told the crowd that just as they could tell what the weather was going to do by watching the sky, so they needed to be aware of spiritual signs and read them too. We are too prone only to condemn without trying to see what promised land God may be leading us to.

Often the good and bad are bound together in a ball. To sort out one from the other is delicate work requiring balance and prayer. Again, it requires discernment to see where good has resulted from something bad. It may be in the form of reaction or standing out against the evil.

Did Jacob realize the fear
he felt was caused by love?
Such awesome love will devastate
our sense; and yet
to feel it is our common way
to love. Moments of ecstasy,
standing upon life's shore,
hearing the harmonies
of heaven's close embrace
borne on the wind,
remind us of another world.
Yet God is here, *the very*
breathing of the world,
the source, the presence, labour's pains,
the joy of all existence. He walks
down the steep paths of history
with us. In him humanity can find
its meaning, energy and love.

Bibliography
A selection

Carmichael, Alexander, *Carmina Gadelica: Hymns and Incantations*, ed. C. J. Moore. First published 1992; reprinted Edinburgh: Floris Books, 1994.

Davies, Oliver, and Fiona Bowie, *Celtic Christian Spirituality*. London: SPCK, 1995.

Eliade, Mircea, *The Sacred and Profane: The Nature of Religion*, trans. W. R. Trask. London: Harcourt Brace, 1968.

Ignatius of Loyola: for the text of the *Spiritual Exercises* and other writings, see *Saint Ignatius of Loyola: Personal Writings*, translated with introductions and notes by Joseph A. Munitiz and Philip Endean. London: Penguin, 1996.

Lawrence, D. H., 'Snake', quoted in *The Faber Book of Modern Verse*, ed. Michael Roberts, revised by Donald Hall. London: Faber and Faber, 1965.

Low, Mary, *Celtic Christianity and Nature*. Edinburgh: Edinburgh University Press, 1996.

MacDonald, George: see the chapter on MacDonald in Newell, *Listening for the Heartbeat of God*.

Newell, J. Philip, *Listening for the Heartbeat of God*. London: SPCK, 1997.

Bibliography

O'Donoghue, Noel: see James Mackey (ed.), *An Introduction to Celtic Christianity*, Edinburgh: T. & T. Clark, 1995.

Teilhard de Chardin, Pierre, *The Heart of the Matter*. London: Collins; and New York: Harper, 1960. For general reading on Teilhard, and the 'Hymn to Matter', see *Pierre Teilhard de Chardin: Writings*, selected with an Introduction by Ursula King. Maryknoll, NY: Orbis, 1999.

Tyrrell, George, *Nova et Vetera*. London: Longmans, Green & Co., 1901.

Waal, Esther de, *A World Made Whole*, London: Fount, 1991.